Violets & Vines

Deborah Marshall

Matador
9 Priory Business Park
Kibworth Beauchamp
Leicestershire LE8 0RX, UK
Tel: (+44) 116 279 2299
Fax: (+44) 116 279 2277
Email: books@troubador.co.uk
Web: www.troubador.co.uk/matador

ISBN 978 1780884 165

British Library Cataloguing in Publication Data.
A catalogue record for this book is available from the British Library.

Typeset by Troubador Publishing Ltd, Leicester, UK

Matador is an imprint of Troubador Publishing Ltd

Printed and bound in the UK by TJ International, Padstow, Cornwall

Violets and Vines is dedicated to the two most influential people in my life:

My Husband, and my Dad.

I love you both so much for all that you are.

CONTENTS

FOREWORD

The blossoming vines spread their fragrance.
Arise, come, my darling; my beautiful one, come with me.
Song of Songs 2:13 NIV

I first met my wife towards the end of 2000, and at that time I would suggest that she was more like a fragile, shrinking violet, than the fruitful vine she has since become. Much of her confidence had long since left her, which had resulted in her being timid and afraid of almost every predicament. I could see from the beginning that there was a much different person craving to emerge from within that delicate outer appearance. However, as I got to know her more, it was clear that her confidence was even more damaged than I had first considered.

It was several years before any real sign of strength and transformation materialised, and this only began to emerge through overcoming incredible heartache, and a virtual mental break down. In the early days of our relationship, she would sink into deep, dark, moods over the most trivial criticism, which would often result with several days of her punishing herself and feeling worthless and ashamed. These moods were incredibly difficult to deal with, as I needed to be extremely careful of the things I suggested in my efforts to build her up. She would fight back at me angrily, but mostly she was fighting with herself. She was completely eaten up with guilt and worry, and often there were no words that I could offer her that would help to rationalise her thinking. For much of the time it was obvious that she honestly wanted to be in a better place. But any repair could be destroyed by the smallest of setbacks, as she battled with the burden of unnecessary guilt and fear.

I eventually persuaded her to have counselling, and, as it turned out, this became a turning point in her healing. Her dad disagreed with this idea completely. "Get her back to church," he told me, "She'll get all the counselling she needs there!" But in those days her guilt was so deep that she would not even consider the idea of going to church, and was convinced that God would be as ashamed of her as she was of herself.

The counselling proved to be a great help, and highlighted many things to her which her troubled mind had chosen to forget. Gradually, she found the courage to go to church and seek God's guidance, and from there the real signs of new growth began to appear. Even then, it was still a slow and delicate process, which regularly highlighted many hurdles for her. However, as the new shoots slowly appeared, they gradually managed to overpower the dead wood that had been prevalent before.

Even today she can occasionally lapse, and her self confidence will take a slide. However, these periods are now much fewer and far between, and she has learned to temper them with a more rational thought trail, therefore creating a better sense of self-belief. She has a network of friends who love her unconditionally, and I believe she has finally discovered how to love herself. Her relationship with God is also unconditional, and has been a powerful tool whenever she has needed to turn over soil, or prune away parts of her life that no longer bear fruit.

Writing ***Violets and Vines*** was by no means an easy task, and it took almost ten years to complete. She had never had the desire to take on such a challenge, which meant that there were times when she lacked the discipline and other skills required to complete her manuscript. However, since this was undoubtedly a plan which God had put His hand on, she honoured the task with the necessary obedience. During the years of writing and re-writing she became increasingly aware of His presence as everything developed. In addition, she learned that as she wrote and brought the whole work together, she was able to forgive many people and situations of her past, and, with that she also discovered an insurmountable sense of healing.

I am as proud of ***Violets and Vines*** as my wife. She understands how far she has grown, and what she has learned about herself through writing it. For me however, I love that she now appreciates how her circumstances when we first met, are far more prevalent in the everyday lives of ordinary women (and men) like her. With this understanding, her hope for ***Violets and Vines***, is that others will be encouraged to make strong decisions that will lead them into a brighter future.

Malc Marshall

You can email Deborah directly at:

violetsandvines@btinternet.com

ACKNOWLEDGEMENTS

I will give you thanks in the great assembly;
among throngs of people I will praise you.
Psalm 35:18 NIV

I have read many books which donate a page at the beginning to list all the people who have in some way helped the author to achieve their dream and turn their book into a reality. I too have been shown a great deal of support and encouragement on my long journey. Many of my friends read through parts of chapters at one time or another and have helped me to get the details right.

As I moved forward on my journey, I found that my mind began to switch off from some of the struggles that I had held on to for many years, and I gained strength in a new confidence as well as freedom to live as the person I really am. Such liberation and confidence helped me to focus on what was happening in my life in the present instead of holding on to what was past, and as a consequence, it became difficult at times to fully remember how this had at one time affected my mental health in such a damaging way.

From a long list of all who have stood by and encouraged me on my way, particularly when I had been running scared like a frightened rabbit, two people in particular have risen above all others. They have been witness to some of my dreadful moods through panic and confusion, and have listened to my fears and revelations over and over as I have had to work through many changes in my life.

Carole Jenet became my friend just as I began to write. Our friendship undoubtedly came via Divine Intervention, and that story alone could be the making of another book! I was undoubtedly taken out of my comfort zone when God told me to write ***Violets and***

Vines, however, this wonderful woman came into my life at the perfect time and took on the role of initial editor as well as offering endless support and encouragement to me during times when I frequently felt as though I were swimming in muddy waters. Often I was in such a hurry to put everything down that it came out muddled and confusing. Carole's subtle edits have given clarity and simplicity to some situations which appeared quite complex as I transferred them from my head to paper. I am intensely thankful for the wonderful work that shc has donc in helping to make ***Violets and Vines*** an inspirational read.

Secondly, I would like to pay tribute to my amazing husband. He has taken the brunt of my moods more than anyone as he gently helped me to emerge from a 'shrinking violet' into the 'fruitful vine' that I have become. When I first told him that I believed God was telling me to write ***Violets and Vines,*** I expected him to laugh and tell me it was all in my imagination. Instead, and without hesitation, he agreed that I had something worth writing about, and that I could do it! Even when, after two years, I heard God tell me to start all over again he gave me his full support as I stood looking up from the bottom of a steep hill for the second time. He has read each chapter over and over many times, and continues to remind me of how far I have come and how I have changed for the better. He shows me unconditional love and believes in all of my dreams, giving me confidence to follow them. Thank you sweetheart, I love you, Stars and Sand.

INTRODUCTION

We have different gifts, according to the grace given us. If a man's gift is prophesying, let him use it in proportion to his faith.

Romans 1:6 NIV

During 2002, Malcolm, who was then my partner was the President of RETRA (the National Trade Association for Independent Electrical Retailers). It was a prestigious position that would last for twelve months, and during that time we had the wonderful privilege of travelling the length and breadth of the country and mixing with many other independent retailers and manufacturers within the industry.

One particular evening, I was staying with him at a hotel in London, and while he attended an industry meeting I chose to stay behind and indulge in the luxurious bath in our room and then relax in the bar with a glass of wine and a book.

The bar was busy and a young female pianist was playing and singing soft, smoky, love songs in the background. It created a gentle, peaceful atmosphere and I found it difficult to pay attention to my reading as I became mesmerised by the ambience and the people drifting in and out of the bar. I have always been fascinated by watching people and wondering about them. I imagine who they are with and think about the way they are dressed, or why they are there, etc. I consider the sort of lifestyles they might have and, on that particular evening, there were many different types of people wandering in and out. My thoughts began to drift towards the pianist. She was in her mid-twenties and played the piano well. She was attractive with a lovely singing voice, and reminded me of my own daughter who at that time was also a singer. From as far back as I can remember, the only thing my daughter ever talked about wanting to do when she grew up was to sing. She had never faltered from that aspiration and had all the talent and personality she needed to be successful. This type of venue would have suited her well and I began to imagine her standing beside the piano with a microphone in her hand.

As I reminisced over my daughter and applauded the pianist on completing each song, my thoughts wandered further still. I considered how we are all gifted in our own individual and personal ways. The singers and entertainers of the world, like the pianist and my daughter, have their roles to play. Their talents bring joy to the people who listen to them. Then there are teachers who use their skills to educate our children and students. Fire fighters, doctors or nurses, all are individually talented and trained in their field, and each of them have a specific and important role within our society.

Almost abruptly I realised how deep my thoughts had trailed, and I reflected on the many changes my life had taken in recent months. For the last twenty years, during my marriage to Anthony, my first husband, I had been contented as a wife and a mother to my two beautiful children. I had no desire to take up a career during those years of nurturing, since parenting and running a home had fulfilled me enough. However, as the children had grown and developed into young independent people, I had gradually recognised a void within my marriage. A void which had been somewhat dormant or perhaps unrecognised within my consciousness for many years, since I had placed all of my energies into my role as a mother, and avoided the worrying issues of my flagging marriage.

The last two years that Anthony and I were together were at best exhausting, at times soul destroying and at worst frightening. Finally admitting such an emptiness within our marriage and that things were not as they should be, I then used every possible idea I could think of to try to put things right and build back the love and intimacy that had become so distant.

However, after months of humiliating knock-backs from my

attempts and what seemed as though it were only me who was fighting to save our relationship, I concluded that we were no longer swimming the same tide and that we each wanted different things. Such a realisation left me examining every aspect of my life as it was, with the hope that I would discover something that would lift my self-esteem and eliminate much of the confusing thoughts I seemed to live with day-to-day.

At around the time that I reached forty, I appeared to wake up from a deep sleep. Realising I needed to make major constructive changes to my life, I looked at where I was and what I had and, despite having no idea what I was looking for, I knew that I would no longer find it in the situation I was trapped in. With more mental strength than I could ever have even imagined I possessed, I made the courageous decision to end my twenty year marriage and begin the search for whatever would make me happy and fulfil me again. As I reached that conclusion, I had no idea where I would initially go or how things might pan out, but for my own self-preservation, it was a decision I had to stick to.

Eighteen months later, I had a new and exciting relationship with Malcolm, the man who was to become my second husband. We shared many common interests and strived for the same things in life. Most importantly, we had recently handed our lives to God, and were aware that our lives had been enriched greatly by making that commitment. With God we were learning to overcome many of the hurdles that had seemed too high for either of us to jump before. I was conscious that He was at work within us both and I was happy for Him to take more control in the way we lived.

* * *

The pianist was still playing as my thoughts shifted and I considered my own talents. If I believed that we have all been delivered our own individual gifts, then I needed to understand what mine were. I am not a singer like my daughter and neither do I have the ability to teach or nurse. I don't have the physical strength to tackle fires or chase criminals, but I can write. God has graciously provided me with the wonderful gift of stringing words together.

Life may have led me down a number of dark and lonely roads at times, but however dark they have been, I have always come through them stronger, though often not without incredible pain and heartache. I have suffered depression, low self-esteem and have been bullied and controlled over a long period. In spite of that, I have survived and with a greater strength than I gave myself credit for at the time.

It occurred to me that evening, as I delved further into my thoughts, that if I was able to express on paper some of my experiences, as well as how I had managed to work through depression almost alone at times, I could possibly inspire any reader who has suffered in a similar way. The pressure building inside me that evening in the hotel bar is not something that I can explain easily, but I know that God was speaking to me, and encouraging me to write this book. My work has been driven by a force which is greater than I am able to understand. The pages that follow include details of some of my most difficult experiences and how I overcame them. I have tried to be honest, while at the same time I have been conscious not to be over daunting with my own story. Instead, I have asked that The Lord would help me to use words that will encourage, and inspire, when hope seems distant.

★ ★ ★

When I first had the calling to write ***Violets and Vines***, I was still greatly encompassed in the depths of despair from the traumatic and emotional dilemmas of my first marriage. I had begun a healing process with the support of my family, but that process was to take much longer than I could have imagined. I was so sure that God was asking me to put the book together, that I threw myself into it feet first. I began work almost immediately and poured out years of pent up anger, fear and pain. I believed that what I was writing was His plan, and therefore it would be helpful to other women who had shared similar experiences to me. The consequence of that was that I spent almost two years trying to write a 'self-help' book for other people's benefit, when I wasn't healed enough myself! Although I had made great strides in repairing the wounds from previous years, I had yet to dig into the roots of them. Subsequently, my 'book' had become an opportunity for me to offload my own emotions instead of it being the inspiration for other people that I had intended and that God wanted it to be.

Such an exercise did have its benefits for my recovery, since offloading onto paper so much of what had happened to me was a therapeutic programme that I needed to go through. Indeed it is one that I would recommend to anyone. By putting things down onto paper, not only are you able to release the blistering pressure that can be all-consuming, but it also allows you to organise your thoughts constructively and attain a perspective that can otherwise be difficult to see and achieve.

Finally, two years into my writing and after I had managed to gain back a substantial amount of mental strength, I was 'spoken to' again. This time the message was very clear and I discovered how God wanted me to approach my work differently. When I told Malc that the only way to do that was to begin again from scratch, he initially shook his head in disbelief. He had supported me relentlessly through the many hours I had worked on my writing up until that point and initially he was not sure if I would be able to cover everything again. But when God approached me that second time, I was given a very specific approach to use. He had been such a focal part of my healing over the two previous years, and I needed to incorporate the relationship I had developed with Him in my writing. As always, and despite his initial reservations, Malc accepted my new enthusiasm and believed in my calling, giving me total support in my fresh venture. Such support was priceless as I sat at my computer on that first day to begin the whole thing again! With great surprise the plan I began to put together this time was vastly different and easier than anything I had written in my previous attempt. As the first few pages took shape, I discovered that God was walking with me in a garden.

By considering the needs of neglected flower beds and overgrown shrubs, I was able to assimilate how we can tend our lives in a comparable way in order to enrich them and bring them back to fruition.

I still believe it has been important to share some of my past experiences, mainly as example. But with a new strength and direction, I hope that I have created a balance between the negatives and the positive outcome of learning to love myself and therefore repair many of the mental wounds I endured through a process of continued erosion and having my confidence sapped away from me.

I was not born with an abundance of mental or physical strength. There had to have been a bigger force than me alone helping me to overcome the hurdles that were placed in my path. I am an ordinary woman, and though at times the events of my life have been alarming and even extreme, I understand that I am far from alone in the struggles I have faced. The circumstances that I once allowed myself to live with are far more common than I could have appreciated. Women hide in loveless relationships either because they believe they are alone in their circumstances and have nowhere to turn to or because they no longer have enough self belief to recognise that they deserve better. I can affiliate with that completely. One of the first things I discovered whilst experiencing my new freedom was that only in recognising the contentment that came with it was I able to appreciate how miserable I had been for so many years. It was in that discovery that I also realised how much I had missed during those lonely times. At rock bottom with no confidence I relied on my first husband to make excuses for my lack of spirit and sullen moods, never understanding that he was often the reason behind them and the person I had become. When you are told something often enough it is inevitable that in the end you will believe it. If I can learn to accept and overcome my past and all the humiliating negativity that was drip-fed to me for almost twenty years, I know without question there is hope for many.

ROOT TREATMENT

My roots will reach to the water, and the dew will lie all night on my branches.

Job 29:19 NIV

This early chapter is designed to outline vital situations throughout my life that allowed me to be more tolerant towards negative issues rather than addressing them head on. I could not have considered that events which went back to my early childhood were so significant in how I developed later in life, if it had not been for a very patient counsellor who recognised that many of my current characteristics are without doubt the result of issues that I had mentally dismissed a long time ago. With his gentle nurturing I was able to confront those issues and understand the way my character had developed from there on. Without addressing those early situations it would not have been possible to overcome the ones I was trying to deal with at the time. It was with his help that I found a clearer understanding of myself and because of that I became less critical of the way I handled certain situations. No matter how irrelevant our root issues may seem later in life, they need to be addressed in order to understand them fully and to let them go.

★ ★ ★

My birth mother left my dad and me when I was still very small. I know little about what went wrong between them, but I was raised with the greatest love and patience, and it is to my dad's credit that I became the person I am now. From the time I was five years old until I was nineteen, with one brief exception, life was simply about the two of us. I continued to have regular contact with my mother but I sometimes found the visits confusing as I struggled with my loyalties towards my dad and wanting to be with her. Inevitably, the bond between us was never the same as the one I shared with my dad. I loved her, but a maternal connection is one that develops throughout the impressionable years of growing. Since she was not around me for most of that time, that bond never fully manifested itself.

Within a couple of years my mother re-married. She lived with her new husband more than 150 miles away and so I spent only limited time with her during school holidays. Her new husband was a lovely man, and together with two children from his first marriage plus the son they later had together, they became a family of their own. Despite my regular visits I never felt as though I completely belonged with this new family. When I arrived during school holidays, I usually felt as though allowances were being made to accommodate me. Squeezing an extra place at the table, making up a spare bed, etc., didn't create a sense of belonging, which was what I craved. We all got along very well though, and years later I nursed my stepfather through motor neurone disease until he died. Over the years I had become very fond of him, but in those earlier years I often felt let down by my mother, as she appeared to put her energies into the needs of her new family. It was the smallest things that hurt me the most, like the family portrait photographs they had done together, which did not include me, or their annual holidays, again without me, and even my Christmas and birthday gifts were never as extravagant or thought about as those that were bought for the other children. These trivial but relevant issues left me to consider that I wasn't totally a part of their family and subconsciously created the initial feelings of a low self-worth.

Being an only child at home with my dad, I longed to have a brother or sister and often felt lonely. I envied my friends who were from larger families and had both parents living in the same house. Indeed, my best friend through the whole of secondary school was one of six! It was usually chaos at her house, but even so I loved being in the thick of it. Since there were already eight mouths to feed, I think it was often hardly noticed that I spent much of my time there for supper after school. I clung to the idea of my own mother and her new family embracing me in that way, but that never happened in the way I needed it to, and already my confidence was beginning to slide.

But for any shortfalls I may have felt, my dad more than made up for them. It was rare for a man to have custody of a child in those days and at times it was incredibly difficult for him to balance bringing me up with earning enough money to cover the bills. I am aware now that there were occasions when he was enormously stretched financially, but he never allowed me to be worried and I don't consider that I ever went short of anything. He tried to be strict but fair, and in most instances I think he succeeded. He never said a bad word against my mother and I wasn't really aware as to what had caused them to divorce. Only by the time I left my own husband, and I was confiding in him through my heartache, did we finally sit down and talk about his divorce more openly. I discovered that although my mother had left us when I was about five or six, she had also left us a couple of times before, when I was very small. It was only in that discovery that I realised that I never remembered her leaving, but I did remember her coming back at least once. I came home from school and she was sitting in the armchair. I hadn't seen her for several weeks, and I rushed over to her and knelt on the floor hugging her legs.

"Go up the sweet shop and get me some cigarettes," she said, but she must have seen my hesitation at leaving her, because she quickly stroked my hair saying, "It's okay, I'll still be here when you get back."

Such disruptions must have been difficult for my dad at the time, as he could not be sure how long she would stay and whether he would need to make arrangements for me to be looked after while he went to work, and of course it was equally confusing for me as a small child. Children are known to be resilient. But they crave security, and as long as they can find that from somewhere, they are usually able to overcome what life delivers, however traumatic. Unfortunately, such resilience is often on the surface and internal scars can be deep and unseen.

A couple of years after my mother left us, my dad met a divorced woman with two children of her own. Very soon we all moved into a new home together in a completely new area. Children can be perceptive, and I remember that I never liked her. At best she made me feel uncomfortable, but mostly she frightened me with her obvious dislike for me, and with the furious arguments she picked for no apparent reason with my dad. In the end it became obvious that this woman had mental health issues. But for two or three years, dad and I were subjected to regular frightening situations. The fights between them were often physical and intense. On more than one occasion I remember her brandishing a bread knife at him and I still have visions of the two of them rolling on the kitchen floor, with him desperate to take control of the knife and her just as desperate to use it. She stabbed him on the forehead with the heel of her shoe and even jumped from the bathroom window while we three children watched from our playhouse. Another time, she poured freshly boiled water from the kettle directly onto her chest and then wandered around the house topless the following day displaying the raw wound. When she wasn't being physically violent, she could be equally as spiteful with nasty comments or using words that I was too young to understand. Once I remember her telling me that my mother was a prostitute. She just blurted it out for no reason. My mother could have been accused of many things, but she was not a prostitute. Because I had never heard that word before, it frightened me, making me feel that she was something very bad. Those were the days of the troubles in Northern Ireland, and the word 'Protestant' was always on the news. I confused this with the word 'prostitute' and became very afraid that my mother had connections with the IRA and Northern Ireland and feared that the Catholics would try to kill her!

The traumas of that earlier period clearly had their effect on me as I became an adult. In fact, this was the crucial issue that the counsellor picked up on when he was trying to bring me to my root issues. That very painful process became a tremendous implement in helping me to finally face and overcome the pain I had buried more than thirty years before. I was able to recognise for the first time that many of my negative characteristics are a direct result of that time.

When we experience a weakness in character or a pattern of behaviour that can leave us vulnerable, it is often the result of an event that happened at an equally vulnerable time in our life. To overcome the pain, we sometimes manage to shut off from it and often we can actually convince ourselves that it never happened at all. Although I have many memories of the violent outbursts I witnessed in my childhood, I also accept that there is still a vast amount that my brain has chosen to deny. Through counselling, many of those forgotten issues surfaced, but I also accept that there are as many more which remain locked in the mysterious vaults of my mind.

Through the careful counselling during the early stages of my marriage break up, I learned that those experiences during my childhood had developed a need for me to be responsible whenever things go wrong in my life. By seeing how my dad hurt and struggled to keep any amount of sanity and normality in my life at that time, even in my infancy, I took on the burden of guilt and blame for all the things that weren't right. My dad's earlier partner abused me both physically and mentally and when he questioned her in any way, she blamed me for coming between them. I tried to keep out of the way in my bedroom, because I feared that the 'wrong' I was doing was the cause of the violent outbursts that flared up between them. I learned to despise myself and believed that I was responsible and deserved everything I got, while at the same time I had a desperate need to feel loved. Gradually as my confidence weakened, the only person who loved me unconditionally was my dad. Therefore I had an urgency to protect him. When I felt unable to do that, along came the guilt. Guilt has been the most significant hindrance of my entire life. As soon as things have gone wrong or broken down, I have crawled into my shell and embraced myself with its comfort.

Finally, by the time I was about twelve, we were spared any more abuse when that dreadful, unstable woman left us quite abruptly. Once again dad never discussed with me what happened to her, but when we came back from our summer holiday that year she was gone. I remember the relief at realising that dad and I would be on our own again and there would be no more violence in our home.

We spent the next seven years together on our own and dad brought me through all the typical issues of adolescence and explaining to me many of the things that a mother would normally undertake. I was so close to him that I had no inhibitions when it came to needing to know about personal issues such as my monthly periods and discussing sex and relationships with boys, etc. Then when I was eighteen he met and subsequently married his soulmate. In the short term this proved to be a delicate and difficult situation for both his new wife and me as we strived for his attention. It caused no end of arguments and resentment towards each other initially, which must have been heartbreaking for my dad at the time. I am not sure when we actually worked out our differences and became confident enough of his individual love for us, but she became an incredible friend to me over time. I love her greatly now, she is the mum I had missed while I was growing up, and with her own four children and the grandchildren that have subsequently arrived (as well as great-grandchildren for mum and dad), I am at last part of a big family!

Over the years, I believed that I had emerged from the earlier period in my childhood unscarred. However, the damage to my confidence was deep though not obvious. As I developed psychologically I was able to forgive my earlier step-mother for all that had happened, because I accepted that she was not mentally stable and therefore not in complete control of her actions. Even so, the scars from those regular outbursts and being witness to such violent fights had clearly manifested within me. Outwardly I appeared unaffected and could not recognise the damage. Inwardly however, the low self-esteem was already eating away at me as I concluded that I had been abandoned by my mother and then rejected by my stepmother. Effectively these negative feelings played a huge part in the relationships I formed in life, and particularly the one with my first husband.

★ ★ ★

Many of us will have been blessed with a wonderful caring family or friends who can offer us good counselling and support as we begin to address painful or delicate issues that normal life brings to us. Their relentless support is a valuable instrument towards our long-term healing. When relationships with other members of our family are fragile though, it can be more difficult to open up and outside counselling becomes another valuable option.

Whoever we choose to confide in, the power behind offloading and sharing our troubles is in itself an influential healing implement. 'A problem shared is a problem halved' is a true phrase and we should not treat it as a cliché. Keeping our problems all to ourselves allows them to overload us with the pressure from negative thoughts and feelings. When we only have ourselves to toss things over with we become restricted to one limited opinion. Such a limit will inevitably hinder our chances of being able to progress and move forward. Sharing in confidence with a person that we trust grants us an instant pressure release, and also creates an opportunity to see a different perspective other than our own.

And there is even more good news because however desperate a situation might seem at the time, or however difficult it is to believe, it almost always comes with a solution. Counselling, whether it be professional or simply sharing with our loved ones, will eventually reveal this to us. Depending on the depth of the scars, it can take longer for some than for others to reach such a conclusion, but nobody need ever be without hope. Mostly the answers are actually straightforward but for the person with no self-esteem or in the depths of depression, it may not seem that way at the time. Often, the healing process can take as long as the damage took to manifest in the first place (and in some cases even longer). Good, long term healing should not be expected to be a 'quick fix'. By papering over the cracks of a problem we leave ourselves exposed to the inevitability of them resurfacing again at any time in the future. The only sure way of avoiding these recurrences is to get to the very root of the problem and treat it accordingly!

* * *

It was after my marriage break-up and when I was first living with Malc that I reached my lowest point. His efforts to pick me up as I sank further and further into depression were impossible for him to manage by himself, and in his desperation to help me he suggested that I would benefit from counselling. Still guilt-stricken from abandoning my first marriage, I was convinced that he had an ulterior motive for wanting to convince me that I was not the awful person I believed I was! Of course his real, motive was only to bring me back to myself and the person he was sure I could be. In such a negative state of worthlessness, it is sometimes easier and makes more sense to place the blame on yourself for everything that goes wrong in your life, and that is exactly what I did. No matter how many times Malc tried to talk my problems through with me, I always managed to convince myself that he had got it all wrong. I would fight back with my own arguments to his rational suggestions, convincing myself that the mess I was in was my own fault. I could not see his reasoning and much of the time I didn't want to.

By the time he booked the counselling session, the pressure of living with so much guilt had overburdened me and I was heading for a complete breakdown. It was a situation I hated to be in, but one I seemed unable to change. I had no reason to be that low other than the fact that I was willingly suffocating myself with my own guilt. In contrast to the traumatic relationship with my first husband, I now had a man who adored every bone in me. He was fulfilling every dream I had ever had and lavished me with love and affection, which was something I had not been used to. He was steady and secure, both financially and emotionally, and he loved me without judgment or criticism. Despite so many positives, I chose to concentrate on my own negatives and consumed myself with blame for the life I had left behind.

Malc says that I reached a point where I seemed prepared to give up on everything I had. He watched me lose interest in all that I valued: our home, my relationship with him and even myself. At that time I didn't even have the desire to get out of bed in the morning, and remember consciously not brushing my hair for two days in an attempt to rebel against his endless efforts to lift me. At one point, for at least two or three days, he spent all of his time going up and down the stairs and tenderly stroking me, loving me and sometimes not even speaking because he simply had no idea what to say. I either argued or ignored anything he did say and so there were times when he was too afraid to talk at all. Half of me was happy when I was ignored, while in contrast I hated feeling so alone. But there seemed no point in conversing with him because he had an opposing opinion against every point I made. I believed he had no idea of how I was feeling and I felt unworthy of his love and efforts. And yet if he had chosen to give up on me and aid my self-destruction, I would have been devastated. Despite my protests and self-pity, I needed him and wanted to be with him more than I could ever remember wanting to be with anyone. But I didn't believe I deserved him.

Initially, when we were first together, I had been completely open with him about the events of my past. I hid nothing from him, so there was nothing that he was unaware of. However, gradually the pressure of actually living the tranquil life I had craved for became more than I was able to cope with while I was consumed by my guilt, and the only way I could deal with it was with self-destruction. I was good at that. I was totally conscious of what I was doing and often purposely twisted Malc's words of encouragement and threw them back at him. I am ashamed to admit that watching his frustration gave me a sense of satisfaction as I knew that I was dragging him down too. Mostly I would tell him that he didn't understand what I was going through because his own life had always been so balanced. This was nothing more than an excuse and far from true. Having nursed his beautiful wife through terminal cancer four years earlier, he could have told me a few stories about reasons to feel depressed and feeling there was little to live for. Julie was thirty-eight years old when she died. Losing her was pain I had never known, but Malc had dealt with his grief with dignity. He didn't feel guilty because he had found love again, instead he recognised the importance of moving forward, which is what he wanted to do with me.

My depression had become so deep that it was numbing the real pain. Although in my heart I hated to be in that state and hated even more what it was doing to Malc, it didn't hurt so much while I was in that condition. In that sunken state, I could dismiss anything that became too painful. It was a hideous place, but it relieved me from pain and heartache that I was not able to address at that time.

Booking the counselling sessions was a last resort for Malc. He had exhausted all ideas to try and help me but knew that he could not allow me to fester like that forever. When the day arrived for me to go he wasn't even sure that I would get out of bed. And neither was I. Only at the very last minute did I get up and throw on some clothes in an act of defiance. As I got dressed, I remember thinking that it would be a good thing to go because then I could prove to Malc that even counselling would not help me. I had been for counselling once before while I was still with Anthony, and I knew that their tactics are to leave you to try and work things out in your own mind, and as far as I was concerned I had already done that.

However, after only one session I could see that this important opportunity to be as open and honest as I had ever been with anyone other than Malc had been a great release. I was right, the counsellor did little of the talking, instead he picked up on the things I told him and prompted me to share more with him. Because he was impartial, I found it easier to accept his advice rather than assume he was merely being kind and sympathetic. I gained much more from those visits than just mental offload. I soon recognised that I had burdened myself unnecessarily and had consequently been putting my life on hold.

In the depths of depression it is understandable to feel incapable of finding answers by yourself. With the patience and understanding of a properly trained counsellor or someone who you can trust to offer you an unbiased opinion, you can gradually make sense of things and slowly work towards unravelling your issues. Having a neutral opinion during a time when your own head is completely muddled will carefully assist you into seeing things from a different perspective and with greater clarity. Once you are able to think rationally, it is surprising and reassuring how different things can appear.

During those early days of my healing, my head was so mixed up it was impossible to think about what groceries I needed, let alone the serious issues of my failed marriage and whether I had made the right decisions. But the professional help and unfailing support of the people who love me most gradually taught me how to love and accept the person I am. I don't say for one minute that it was easy. I shed more tears through my recovery than I ever did during my dark days. It was a slow and painful process that took almost four years to achieve and even today I still have to work at keeping a positive attitude at times. However, for the first time that I am able to remember I am finally free from the years of unnecessary guilt that imprisoned me for so long.

Having managed to treat the 'root issues', I have discovered an inner peace that comes only with acceptance. Accepting yourself for who you are. Accepting the past as something you cannot change. Accepting that you are in control of your own decisions and choices, and accepting that you are not necessarily responsible for every negative aspect in your life. But most importantly for me, it has been about accepting that whatever experiences I have had and despite all the mistakes I may have made in the past (and for those that I shall make in the future), God still loves me, and He forgives me. By accepting that, I have learned that there is little else that I need.

THE WEEDS AND THE WORMS

As the weeds are pulled up and burned in the fire,
so it will be at the end of the age.
Matthew 13:40 NIV

Once the soil had been forked over and the roots were disturbed, the worms came out. They were countless. Many were small and threadlike while others had been churning away under the surface for years and were much larger. Virtually all of them related to the exhausting realisation that my marriage to Anthony had at times been harrowing even though in my own mind I had concluded that much of the misery and despair I had endured was 'normal'. Crawling in and out of my mind and weaving through the weeds and fragile roots that had only recently been overturned, they consumed me as individually I attempted to address them. Some had embedded themselves over several years and though in the beginning they had been nothing more than small grubs, over time as they had been allowed to develop and mature they had been the driving force in draining me of my confidence and self-esteem.

With the roots exposed, the weeds were ready to join forces with the worms in an effort to bring me to my knees. Already they had almost achieved that as I plunged into such a deep state of depression that even Malc found himself in his own pit of frustrated helplessness in his attempts to pull me back again. His desperation to do this and to bring me back to the person he had already seen in me had had little effect and he became lost in an anxiety of his own that slowly drained him of all ideas to achieve this. He didn't deserve to be treated as unfairly as I treated him during those times. All he wanted was someone to love and for them to love him back. But in the depths of negativity I was unable to love myself let alone give him the love that somewhere very deep within me I wanted to share with him. Knowing how fragile I was and accepting there was another person trying to escape from inside myself, he relentlessly supported me and patiently waited for my strength to be restored, understanding that he could do little more than to listen and share my infantile joy each time the counsellor helped me to make another clear discovery in my head.

There were more than thirty years worth of weeds and worms surfacing to the forefront of my mind for the first time, and it took incredible strength to separate them and free myself from their spaghetti-like tangle. Counselling was the only way I could have unravelled such emotional demons but since I had been drowning in despair, it had fallen on Malc to take my hand and lead me in that direction. As each day passed and my mind was churned over, a clearer picture of my past existence became apparent. Even with such a picture developing it was incredibly difficult to shake away the guilt and overwhelming feelings of responsibility that had always gone hand in hand.

My out of character behaviour could only be excused as I came face to face with the unsettling and painful issues of my childhood for the first time with the mind of a grown person. When my memory had closed off from my problems all those years before, I had been a small and immature child. As an adult, the picture was completely different from the one I had left behind. I was almost the frightened little girl again. I could feel the torment in that child's face and wanted to protect her and free her from her fears and confusion. She needed to be embraced with security and reassurance that the torments she had endured were not her fault. As that little girl I just wanted to be loved.

When the painful and confusing memories unravelled more of what had been hidden away, my energy levels drained further still and my brimming reservoir of tears seemed unwilling to dry up. For days I cried and cried until my eyes were sore and my body shattered. Although I had now progressed from the depression of staying in my bed all day, I was consumed with the need to discuss the many stories that were coming together with clarity for the first time. It was incredibly frightening as I opened up and discussed so much with Malc to discover more and more about my past and the person I had become because of it. Even so I could feel a safety valve unscrewing itself and for the first time in my life I was able to take an understanding that many of the things that had happened had not always been 'normal' and that most of the guilt I had burdened myself with was not my fault.

Only once the clarity started to take shape and some of the fear subsided was I able to look toward the next chapter in my healing. Those original traumatic problems of the past amounted to two obvious incidents in my early childhood: my mother leaving me, and the abuse I had been subjected to from my stepmother. The current issues were an accumulation of mental torments that had drowned my confidence in a lengthy drip-feed process over many years since then. In retrospect, those early incidents had had a significant effect on the way I had then formed relationships, particularly during my impressionable adolescent years.

As a teenager during the time when my dad and I were living on our own, I had switched off from all that had happened in my earlier childhood. Clearly my dad was aware of the impact my stepmother had had on me, but in our new situation, once we were on our own again, he created our home into a stable environment where I felt safe. Though he was strict he was never volatile, and I was able to dismiss the fear of the violence I had known before. I became a happy teenager and my friends were always keen to visit my house, as my dad was easy going with a good sense of humour. I was a bit slow in having boyfriends, which was mainly down to confidence and I tended to be a bit timid on my own in their company, but the good sense of humour I inherited from my dad made me popular and confident in a group situation.

At eighteen I met my first love, Alan. We were both the same age and the relationship developed quickly between us. I celebrated my nineteenth birthday with an engagement party and shortly after began planning a wedding. Neither of us had been in a serious relationship before, which made our plans all the more exciting. Each month we saved money to build a deposit for a house and where before I had spent my money on clothes and cosmetics I began to enjoy buying soft furnishings instead.

During the summer of that year, while my dad was away on holiday, I held a party at home for my friends, including my fiancé. It was at that party that Alan and I had our first major row, when I discovered him embracing another girl. I was devastated and after another more heated argument the following day, he hit me for the first time. I should have walked away then but instead I chose to forgive him and listened to his pathetic excuses with sympathy. I considered that I needed to accept my share of the blame for the argument and that he had only lashed out at me in his frustration. Therefore it wasn't all his fault. That sympathy and forgiveness had given him a licence to hit me again and again each time we argued after that. The pattern for our future had already been established.

Alan appeared to be a quiet, inoffensive character. He had been a model student at school achieving the highest grades and later gained a place at university. He was generally popular, so when I tried to discuss his aggression with my friends they found it hard to believe me. I didn't want to leave him, I just wanted him to stop hitting me. I didn't want to throw our plans away and I was sure there was a way I could stop the fights. He only ever seemed to lash out at me if he had been drinking and I stupidly believed that if I could keep him sober I could change everything and the fights would stop.

Unfortunately, Alan continued to drink and often did it to gain the confidence he needed to strike out at me. No matter how I tried to approach him in order to avoid a confrontation, the violence escalated. During our second Christmas together, he knocked me to the floor, kicked me in the ribs and slapped me on the back with such force that I was left with a bruise in the shape of his splayed hand. As was normal after such a fight, he crawled around me pathetically apologising for what had happened. In my heart I knew it wasn't my fault, but still allowed myself to be burdened with some of the blame. Though I hated the fighting, it sometimes crossed my mind that such behaviour was normal between two adults, as I had seen it before when I was a child. But somewhere in the pit of my soul I knew that this was not how things should be.

After that particularly brutal incident, I decided to spend some time with my birth mother as I did not want to involve my dad with my problems. There was a huge part of me that was concerned he would feel disappointed in my failure in the relationship, and I was also afraid that, despite his easy going nature he might feel urged to retaliate if he were to learn that my boyfriend was abusing me. I thought that spending some time in a different environment would be a welcome break and an opportunity for me to do some straight thinking. I eventually opened up and told my mother what had been happening. Like many of my friends, she saw Alan as a quiet inoffensive lad and her response was for me to get myself home and sort it out, reminding me that we had a wedding to plan! Disappointed doesn't begin to cover my reaction to her advice, and once again I felt she had rejected me without giving enough thought to my needs. There had been few occasions in my life where I had genuinely missed having her around me, and this had been one of them. I desperately needed her support at that time. However, her lack of understanding and unwillingness to stand by me emphasised once more how her life had moved on in another direction from mine. I felt abandoned yet again as I realised I had nobody to turn to.

At that time I had yet to discover the joyful friendship that God wanted to share with me. Since becoming a teenager I had not continued with the regular Sunday school worship that my dad had encouraged when I was a child. Like many adolescents, I had instead chosen to hang out with the 'cool kids' who saw church as an institution for old folks and boring people. Had I continued to develop my relationship with God at an early age, I am sure that many things would have panned out differently and I would have found the support and understanding I needed. In later years a relationship with God would have been an enormous comfort as I encountered even more turbulence during my first marriage.

Believing that I had no one to turn to at that time, I did as my mother had advised and for the next couple of months I tried to work things out with Alan. He was gentle for a while, but my heart was never totally his after the episode at Christmas. There were a further couple of unpleasant incidents after that, though generally they were not as violent. I thought that we had turned a corner and the violence had finally subsided though I remained guarded, as the threat was always apparent even if things appeared to be going well.

One evening while we were at a party he became very drunk. His mood changed quickly and I recognised all the signs that he wanted to pick a fight with me. As soon as we had left the party he became verbally insulting and once we got back to his house I was again subjected to his violent abuse with the same brutal force he had used at Christmas. Just as before, he pitifully apologised afterwards, but I knew then that he had hit me for the last time. I finally realised that this man would never treat me any differently and that our relationship had no future. It was better to leave him before we were married than to risk continued abuse as well as the complications of a divorce in the future. In retrospect, my apprehensions about entering a long-term relationship with Alan were understandable given the insecurities of my childhood. He had no more cause to abuse me than my stepmother had when I was a child. Still, they had both taken advantage of me and I desperately needed somebody to love and protect me other than my dad.

Just a few weeks after I finally made the break from Alan and while I was still running scared and vulnerable, I met Anthony. He appeared to be my knight in shining armour as I explained the violence that I had escaped from and he reassured me that in his eyes hitting women was the lowest of the low. I felt safe with him. He seemed to embrace all my fears and squeeze them out of me. I grew fond of him very quickly in my new safety zone, and we were married just sixteen months after we first met. Anthony appeared to create an environment that gave me all the security that was essential to rebuild my confidence. It was impossible for me to see that I was about to be preyed on again as Anthony slowly took advantage of my vulnerability with a much more subtle approach than I had previously known.

Despite being unaware that I had been affected by my childhood, one thing I feared was being deserted and abandoned again. I fell in love with Anthony very quickly and was convinced that he would look after me and love me. And with that feeling of security I used my own manipulating techniques to make sure that I did not lose him. I set out to be the perfect girlfriend, so that he could not help but love me. I gave him all the attention he desired. I brought him gifts, sent him cards with tender notes on, and when he was posted overseas for six months while serving in the British Forces I wrote to him virtually every day so that he could keep up with the local news, but more to the point to be sure he would not forget me. My efforts paid off and while he was still out there he wrote and proposed to me. It was the happiest time for me believing that I had finally found someone who loved me and quickly turned all my dreams into a false sense of security, as I foolishly believed that I would never be alone again.

* * *

The fallout of these two relationships created an insecure, damaged person who hid behind a wall of self-imposed guilt. As the reality of my shattered past consumed me with the army loads of worms and weeds attempting to break what little confidence I had left, Malc was without doubt my greatest visible strength and defence. It takes a very special person to give unrelenting support and understanding when they are continually knocked back with negative outbursts and abusive retaliations to their efforts. This is precisely what Malc had to cope with as he frequently encouraged me through every emotion I encountered as I learned to understand for the first time how controlled my life had been up until that point.

He had seen me at my lowest. I had spent days in bed with no interest for life outside of my bedroom. Once the counsellor had uprooted the hidden issues and the worms and weeds began their attack, it was difficult for me to think straight for much of the time as they strangled their way inside my head. Even so, on a positive note, I could see my eyes were opening up and recognising many things for the first time. Such therapy had indicated how my character had burdened itself with unnecessary responsibility and guilt. It seemed that my early vulnerability had allowed many of the key people in my life to lay all sorts of responsibility on me. By conditioning myself to it, I readily took it on when things went wrong. It was refreshing to recognise that and, though I did not recover overnight, I was gradually able to find a clear vision and understanding of that burden. Then, one by one and with childlike urgency, I needed to offload and share with Malc all that I discovered. He proved to have just as much patience and understanding to help me then as when I had been depressed and stuck in my bed.

Endlessly I would need him to listen as the child inside me excitedly recognised something else that would release me from my guilt. Again, many things were trivial on their own, but collectively and because they had been manifesting for so many years, they had been the cause of my downfall. He was a wonderful listener and the reassurance that he loved me enabled me to completely open up and trust him with the many secrets that had been locked in the vaults of my mind. He was very aware of how fragile I was and consciously had to calculate his reaction to anything I threw at him. He realised that one wrong answer could have dropped me straight back into the pit I was beginning to climb out of. He was able to appreciate that in advance, and with no background training or even a close friend for him to confide in, he had to learn to treat each situation differently and understand my state of mind at that particular time.

When I reflect on all that he did to encourage and help me find my strength again, it was clearly an act of selfless love. There were occasions when I must have been the most difficult person to understand. I had severe mood swings and often rejected the unconditional love that he wanted to give me, believing I was not worthy of it. There were many occasions when I would not allow him to share my thoughts and fears and discarded his efforts in furious outbursts not so different from the ones I had learned about so well throughout my childhood and first marriage. Despite my negative responses to his efforts, and his own frustrations, he continued to appreciate that there was more to me than I was allowing him to see and thankfully he was not prepared to give up on me. When I ask him now why he tolerated so much from me, he tells me that he could always see my potential!

⋆ ⋆ ⋆

A long way forward from that dark time, I can now recognise how living through and subsequently overcoming the weeds and the worms was an essential part of my healing. Though at times they were overbearing, a wonderful positive result emerged through the pain they initially brought with them. The worms that were overturned through counselling, though incredibly painful and confusing at the time, have given me enormous amounts of long-term strength. It is often said that what doesn't kill you will make you stronger, and there is much truth in that quote. However, I now believe that it is more true to say that God only allows as much adversity as he clearly knows you are able to overcome, and even then He continues to walk alongside you all the way until He is able to reveal inner strength that you may never have been aware of. Through these awful, draining times, though the weeds and the worms attacked me for a while, essentially their exposure created vital nutrients to my undernourished soil.

With the strength I have drawn from my loved ones and the unfailing relationship I have with God, I have discovered that just as the weeds and the worms carry with them essential invisible forces, the silent unseen effects of prayer as well as the vital work of the Holy

Spirit also help to break up the clogged soil of our souls and produce in us those wonderful fruits from the Spirit. (Galatians 5:22-23). God has been with me at all times, and even when I have been unaware of His presence, He has watched me grow through my trials, though He never gave me more to deal with than He knew I could overcome. The weeds and the worms have been valuable lessons that He brought to me for a purpose in order that I can now appreciate the rich soil that has been prepared for the future growth in my life garden. Amen to that.

KNOCK DOWN THE BARRIERS

Thorns had come up everywhere, the ground was covered with weeds, and the stone wall was in ruins.

Proverbs 24:31 NIV

My first husband and I were indisputably two extreme characters. Subconsciously I understood that early into our marriage, but given my low feelings of self-esteem and my fear of being deserted and alone I convinced myself that our relationship was happy and normal. I had used my own method of manipulating in order to win his love, but that did not guarantee me the happiness I yearned for. We were often incompatible because Anthony's needs were usually more important to him than mine, and most of the time I allowed him to fulfil them. Even so I felt safe within the cocoon of my home and my family, and that security compensated for the many disappointments and feelings of neglect I experienced over the years. I was blinded by my need to be loved and secure and as a result I often dismissed my own personal needs as a woman. As we grew deeper into our marriage the security of those years falsely assured me that what we shared was genuine love and compatibility when the reality was that we were at a great distance from each other with many of our interests and morals conflicting.

My obvious neediness allowed Anthony to mould me into a person to suit his own purposes. It was essential for him to have his own independence, regularly playing all types of sport that required him to be away from home for many hours at a time, several times a week. This recreation was not just periodic, it would occupy as many hours as he was able to get away with, and was more important to him than spending good quality time with us all as a complete family. This often left me feeling almost completely responsible for the needs of our two children and I frequently felt like a single parent as their demands together with running the home and trying to shuffle money around to make ends meet were at times too draining and tiring for me to cope with on my own day after day.

In contrast to Anthony spending so much time out of the house, I was a natural homemaker. I wanted to build a stable and loving environment like the one my dad had provided for me. At the same time I also had a desire for him to see that I had done things correctly with Anthony and I raising our children together in a normal family unit. I had gained so much of my experience about running a home and taking care of finances from my dad, and with the recollection of my own broken childhood always apparent I could not contemplate causing a similar situation or allowing anything to come before my home or my family. As each year passed I congratulated myself for the achievement of being married longer than my own parents and for my success at parenting. It was essential to me that my dad should be proud of me, and it was this unrelenting determination that gave me much of the staying power I needed in order to tolerate Anthony's constant periods of selfishness and inconsideration towards his family.

In the beginning, I appeared warm and bubbly on the surface, but underneath I was insecure and afraid of any form of confrontation. When I was disheartened at having to spend another Sunday afternoon without my husband around, I would not usually protest openly. Instead I would stay away from friends and family to hide my depressed feelings. Whilst Anthony was fun loving and outgoing, he also had a quick and violent temper which he frequently used as a weapon in order to secure his own way. I very quickly learned to agree with him in order to avoid having a violent outburst, and he equally quickly discovered how easy it was to control me and leave me at times rigid with fear. In time I was often able to recognise when I had pushed him over the edge and he was about to lose control, but with each violent outburst I grew more and more afraid that one day I would push him too far and that would be the day he would lash out at me just as Alan and my stepmother had. Such a threat of violence was overshadowed though, at the dread of him leaving and the idea that I might end up alone and a single parent.

In contradiction to Alan, Anthony would indirectly take his temper out on everything but me, though these outbursts were no less terrifying than those I had known before. I lost count of the number of times he punched his fists through doors or kicked furniture over. Many dinners ended up against the wall with the plate smashed across the floor. He justified these outbursts by reminding me frequently that even though he lost his temper he never took it out on me physically and I became grateful for that. I therefore wrongly concluded that his violent temper was not as brutal as that which I had been subjected to with Alan. Sometimes I was able to defuse the situation if I managed to back down before he blew his fuse. Instead of standing my corner I would grovel and apologise for causing him to become so angry with me in the hope that my guilt would satisfy him enough to calm down and take on a gentle tone with me once again. Other times I wasn't quick enough and I could only watch in fear as he released his aggression in an uncontrolled rage.

In the midst of these outbursts, and particularly when the children were small, my concerns would be only for their protection and security. I never wanted them to witness violent scenes similar to the ones I had done at their age. Sometimes I would send them to their room while I attempted to defuse things, and other times I would just sit and hold them to offer them security so they would know I was a safe haven for them. I remember once when my son was less than a year old locking both the children in the car while Anthony was throwing cups and screaming in the house. There had been no provocation for that outburst other than my young son crying while his daddy was trying to watch the football on TV! When his rage finally calmed and I brought the children back into the house he walked out carrying his suitcase. I thought he was gone for good but just a few hours later he came back with a box of chocolates and his tail between his legs. My sense of relief that he had come home again was much greater than the earlier fear as he went ballistic in our home, and rather than discuss what had happened earlier, I accepted the chocolates with great relief and forgave him.

The children were often visibly upset but seldom questioned why he had lost control. Both of them were afraid of him at times but like me they would never dare to question him. My sons' insecurities manifested into a fear that his mummy and daddy would divorce, while my daughter did not openly show her fears in the same way. As she got older she sometimes took her chances and attempted to stand up to him. She rarely ever came out on top as he would readily display his aggression towards her in the same way as he did to me in order to install enough fear to make her back down and believe she was the loser in that particular fight.

When the storm had subsided, Anthony and I would often make up with him apologising and comforting me through my tears as he tenderly accepted his responsibility for the outburst. Like a naughty puppy or a scalded child, he would be as gentle as necessary in order to win favour with me again. The children would take comfort in seeing this placid side to their dad as he displayed his affection attentively reassuring all of us that everything was fine. These obvious displays of gentleness were a rare indulgence that allowed me to soak up the affection I craved. Other times there would be no kissing and making up and he would remain cold and quiet until the end of the day. I had learned not to even attempt to approach him on these occasions, since he would warn me with as much threat as he could deliver that I should not speak to him for the rest of the day. He would still be spoiling for a fight and the smallest amount of provocation could blow the whole thing up again.

★ ★ ★

During those controlling years of my marriage as well as all that happened previously, I had allowed everything I had ever faced to stack up in front of me and create a solid wall that separated the person I really was from the one I had become. Since the incidents in my childhood, many people had managed to control my thoughts and I had allowed that rather than risk a conflict. Nobody took more advantage of me in that way than my first husband. It was his mental bullying that continued to eat away at my confidence for many years even after I had left him.

As I gained enough composure to talk in more depth to either Malc or the few people I confidently trusted, one of the most significant words that were used in all their advice was 'manipulator'. Anthony was a first-class manipulator to ensure that he got his own way. I had to do a great deal of research on the subject of manipulation in order to understand for myself just how well he had mastered that skill in our relationship.

At the point when I had decided to leave him and needed to explain things to members of my family and friends, many were amazed at the depth of my unhappiness. Those closest to me were shocked as I unravelled a story of long-term unhappiness and discontent. Most had assumed our relationship to be happy and solid. This was a perfectly understandable conclusion because over the years I had mastered the art of covering my pain by joking at Anthony's lack of consideration towards the children and me instead of allowing my real feelings known.

A manipulator's aggression and tactics are not always obvious to either the victim or their acquaintances. In fact, their strategies are generally subtle as they use the appealing side of their character in order to achieve their own end. They can make it seem as though they are the ones who are being hurt or that they are caring and considerate or even defending you. They will appear to be anything other than fighting or controlling.

In the case of my first husband, I had allowed him to engineer these traits extremely well. Anthony was reputed to have a wonderful sense of humour. He was extremely sharp witted and delighted in playing the joker. He was incredibly good at speaking to people at all levels and it seemed that whatever their needs he was able to appear as though he understood and empathised with them by getting perfectly on their level. This almost always won him favour and was one of the things that had first attracted me to him.

Using that same technique, he was also usually able to convince me that I was wrong even when I felt certain that I was right. So many times I would try to talk to him about a situation where I was confident that I had a valid point only to be persuaded by him that I was wrong and my point had no purpose. I never noticed quite how often he had done that over the years until my daughter began to question me in the same vein when she was in her teens.

"I don't see the point in speaking to dad about it," she would say, "if he doesn't agree with me, he'll only manage to convince me that I'm wrong anyway." On listening to her point, I realised, maybe for the first time, just what a strong character Anthony was and how much he used his strength in order to achieve his own ends. Even then I would still back down and defend him, or I would tell my daughter to do the same and agree with him in order to keep the peace.

All of us have weaknesses and a clever manipulator is able to exploit them to their advantage. Children are first-class at this as they press hard on our guilt button in order to achieve their end. "Please let me have one mummy, I'm the only person in the whole class who doesn't have one yet." So mummy will give in and buy whatever is needed to pacify her child because she cannot bear the idea of her little cherub being the only one in the class to be deprived. At that point she will have no realisation that her child has just taken control of her. Her little treasure however, will have discovered a valuable tool in learning how to twist his mummy round his finger. From then on he will use that skill whenever necessary for his own gain.

Anthony was a master manipulator, though once again through my naivety at the time I was married to him I was unable to recognise just how well he could turn a situation round for his own end. The ***Ask Oxford Online Dictionary*** lists a number of words to describe a manipulator. When I came across words such as *Form, Operate, Shape, Control, Engineer* and *Influence* I recognised those characteristics in him.

But when I read "to control or influence cleverly or unscrupulously", a much clearer picture of my relationship and the man I had loved began to emerge. It was somewhat frightening to discover how much of myself had become lost through fear during the years of my first marriage.

My avoidance of arguments had made it easy for Anthony to impose his strong character on me and exercise his need to be in control to his own advantage. He had used a number of methods to be in command of my thoughts and behaviour yet on the surface appeared a charming and loveable person. He would openly tell anyone and everyone how much he loved me and had no problem in displaying his affections towards me when we were in company. I responded eagerly to those affections since Anthony was not so obvious with his affection and intimacy when we were alone. Added to that I had a great need for other people to see us as the happy and secure couple I wanted us to be. If people saw us as stable and together, then ridiculously it helped to convince me that there was little wrong between us!

As I slowly recognised the extent of the control I had been under over the years, I recollected on many incidents when I had not fully understood what Anthony had been doing at the time and how I had allowed him to rule our marriage. Just a few weeks after we were married a situation arose that should have set alarm bells ringing even then.

Anthony was serving in the British Armed Forces, and I had given up my job to move into our married quarters fifty miles away. It was a particularly lonely time for me, as I had never lived apart from the home I had shared with my dad. Anthony would leave for work at 7.30 each morning and not get home again until 5.30 p.m. It was a long day and with no friends or job, I would spend much of the day just looking forward to him coming home. On this particular day he became upset that his dinner was a few minutes late. He said he had to go straight out again because he had football practice and had a friend waiting for him in the car outside. I had discovered that same day, less than two months into our marriage, that I was pregnant with our first child. This had been unexpected news and I had waited all day for him to come home so that we could discuss the future with our new baby together. When he came home, I tried to sit down with him to talk about it. This meant that dinner was held up for a while, and he then became agitated that he would be late for a planned football practice session with his friends. At my obvious upset, he flew into a rage telling me that he had played football before we were married and he did not intend to change his social calendar just to suit me. In his temper, he suggested that if I was unhappy I should think about going back to live with my dad! He then left the house leaving me in floods of tears. I had not seen that side of his character until that point and felt depressed and deflated as I spent the evening alone with my news waiting for him to return. He came back very late after drinking in the NAFFI with his mates until the bar closed. Staying out late became a regular punishment over the years if I dared to stand up to him or tried to make a point. On a couple of occasions he didn't come home at all, and then in the morning he would walk through the door in total silence still looking irritated or else he would be charming and act as if nothing had happened. I would be too afraid to broach the subject or ask him where he had been all night, just being grateful that he had come home at all.

On the surface that early incident might not appear so unreasonable and as a 'one-off' it would not have been. It became a problem only because my reaction to it gave him a green light for future occasions when he wanted to do something that I might be opposed to. By raising his voice he had already learned that I would back into a corner. Alarmingly, in the same way that I had taken on the guilt with Alan, on these occasions I would convince myself that I was the one being unreasonable for expecting him to stay at home with me instead of considering *his* needs! He often reminded me that he worked hard all day and so he needed recreational time to unwind, and it was unfair of me to invade his well earned valuable time to himself.

In retrospect, it is easy to see the signs but, during those initial days of transition when I was learning to adjust to a new life away from my friends and my dad, I was often overwhelmed by my new circumstances. My pregnancy had not been planned and, with all the other new things that were happening at the same time, my emotions and hormones were in turmoil. Having allowed Anthony to win that first battle I had paved the way for him to win the next one and the one after that. Then without even knowing, he was already taking control of our relationship. The more he got away with, the easier I made it for him. Brick by brick, he was building a wall around my confidence and those early experiences from my childhood were the sturdy foundations it needed to stand on. Gradually, as each brick took its place, a barrier was being built around my character and one that I could hide behind whenever I needed to. Behind the wall most people could not see what was really going on in my life, including myself. The bigger it got, the easier it was to shelter from situations that I was not strong enough to face up to, and the darkness that formed around me sapped more and more at my confidence.

* * *

Hardly anyone will walk life's path without facing a storm or two. Some will stumble

upon one difficult situation after another and gradually each little problem will collectively manifest itself and build a wall before them that will eventually close in and prevent them from seeing anything beyond it. It only takes tiny stones constantly tossed together to create a barrier on top of an existing delicate character.

Getting to the roots of problems is often only the beginning of our healing. Once the roots have been disturbed, all that has been built above them will also need to be considered and carefully addressed. The emotional bricks need to be cautiously knocked down little by little.

It is essential that each one is dealt with thoroughly and

appropriately. To consider taking on the wall and knocking it down with one fell swoop would result in enormous unmanageable amounts of rubble to contend with all at once and risk overlooking many of the key issues which could become lost in the debris instead of tackling them correctly.

It is equally important to acknowledge that when we plant new shrubs in our garden we tend to place them in an area of light with plenty of space to provide every opportunity for them to flourish naturally. Sunlight is essential for their growth as is a gentle rain to nourish the soil. Without exposure to these essential nutrients they will not have the opportunity to develop into the beautiful blossoms that we anticipate and no amount of watering or nurturing will make any difference as eventually they will dry up completely. Equally, we too have the opportunity to develop with rich blossoms, but we need to provide ourselves with good soil and adequate exposure to sunlight as well as space enough to grow. The sunlight will not find us through the cold brickwork of the emotional wall so we must endeavour to break it down. In order to do that, we first need to understand what gives the wall its strength.

Fear is often the biggest hindrance in breaking down barriers. We are often tempted to stay with what we know rather than take a risk on an option that might be a better long-term plan for us. If we don't know something well enough, we are sometimes too afraid to try it. In effect we would rather be certain that we are miserable, than take the risk of being happy!

When a shrub has become limp and lifeless and its strength has been sapped away, it will need to rely on a keen gardener to understand its needs and provide it with essential nutrients to bring it back to itself. By the time we have reached that same depth ourselves we often lack enough physical energy or the courage to fight back on our own and instigate the necessary changes to turn our situation around. Other times, we can be too proud to ask for help and even more often we simply don't recognise the depths that we have sunk to. In my case it was Malc who recognised that I needed outside help and together with the counsellor, they became my gardeners as they began the delicate and lengthy process of gently knocking down one stone at a time until my wall was completely demolished and they could begin to feed me with the essential nutrients I had been denied for so long.

When a wall has been so slowly built that it has taken several years to reach its full height, it can be the most frightening feeling to realise that it needs to come down. Though it may have been a negative drain on our confidence, it will also have acted as a place of refuge to hide behind when things have been overbearing. In order for our lives to progress and move forward from the dreariness of stagnating behind it we have to overcome the fears and anxieties that stand in our way. Not to do this leaves us open to many more years of what has gone before as well as allowing the people who have been involved in its formation to appear even more powerful than they already think they are. But mostly, by choosing to stay hidden we deny ourselves any opportunity to thrive or for our characters to develop into who we really are.

★ ★ ★

There were a number of situations that finally brought me face to face with my wall. Even once I had recognised some of them, the idea of clearing away those heavy stones and creating a clearer path was terrifying. Despite having caught glimpses of all that was beyond it, I didn't have the confidence to choose something that was outside my comfort zone. I was petrified of letting go of all that I was used to. I had reached a point of desperation but was afraid of the alternative choices that I would need to accustom to and was not convinced that they would make a significant difference.

My children had always been the core of my life. That feeling of abandonment from my own childhood was always with me as I raised them and the idea of upsetting their lives in a similar way was unthinkable. As my marriage fell apart, they had reached a point in their own lives where they were stepping out of their children's shoes and making that wonderful transition between child and adult. As teenagers, my relationship with them had changed from childhood neediness into independence, and those two young people had become my friends. I spent quality time with each of them, involving myself in their activities. These were wonderful times and all the energies that I put into being involved with my children allowed me a few hours escapism from the depressing situation that waited for me at home.

It was at the same time that I had found this wonderful friendship with my children that I also reached forty. Having endured the worst time of my marriage during the preceding eighteen months, I subconsciously began to look at my life in a way I had never done before. A few months after my fortieth birthday and with God only a distant ally that I called to in emergencies, He began to make His presence more apparent. Though I had taken regular prayer by myself most days for several years, my pattern of prayer had recently changed from one of begging and bargaining to that of asking for mercy. It was incredible how I began to feel a sense of calm once I altered to that way of talking to Him. For as long as I could remember I had bargained with God by asking Him to deliver us money to overcome one financial dilemma or another, and in exchange I had promised that I would go back to church and really believe! I used to promise God all sorts of things if He would just help us out of our circumstances. Gradually, as I became more and more desperate to our circumstances and, feeling as though I were completely alone, I surrendered myself to Him. Instead of asking for money I simply began to ask Him for His guidance and love. I can remember tearfully telling Him one night that I was lost and needed Him to help me. I wasn't aware of His presence back then, but I know now He was always standing beside me, and I had never been never completely alone.

Quite suddenly, as my prayer path changed, it occurred to me that at forty years old, with God's grace, I might live for many more years and if that were the case I was disturbed to think that the rest of my life could continue on the same path and never be any different. Having nothing else to use as a comparison, I could not be sure exactly what I wanted but I was aware that aside from the relationship with my children there was very little that was fulfilling me. Anthony was continually wheeling and dealing yet never making sufficient money to cover our bills. Consequently, we received regular final notices in the post and were often without basic commodities such as electricity or the phone line. There had been no intimacy in our relationship for as long as I could remember and he appeared to have no desire to change that. Each time I attempted to discuss my fears he either dismissed them by twisting the facts or else he blanked me completely.

So as I turned forty I considered that I was still a relatively young woman and as I accepted that, the gaps in the wall widened and allowed me to recognise for the first time the flaws within my relationship and my life in general. At that time, I believed that I still loved Anthony and since I had spent virtually all of my adult life with him it was inevitable that if the wall were to come down there would be an enormous amount of debris left behind as it hit the ground. It was a tremendously daunting prospect at a time when my confidence was already drained. Nonetheless, I was somehow given the strength I needed to instigate its demolition.

It was not one isolated incident that finally knocked it over. Rather, it was an accumulation of my increased unhappiness added to my fear of getting older and still feeling depressed and unfulfilled. Anthony's refusal to discuss anything with me led me to believe he no longer had enough interest in our marriage to work at rebuilding it, and I did not have the strength to rebuild it on my own. Collectively highlighting all of these considerations had already caused the wall to crumble. There could be no going back.

It is true that when a wall comes down there has to be rubble. However, it is also true that the rubble can be cleaned away. Inevitably it will take time and is bound to be an exhausting operation, but in the end it is usually possible to work through the rubble and find a clear path. It is unlikely that a well established wall can be demolished completely unaided but there is no sin in relying on the pillars of our trusted friends, family or councillors to assist us through its demolition. Then, with an uncluttered path, we can view the road ahead with confidence and optimism. If God can take the ruins and remains of Good Friday and change them into Easter Day, we can achieve anything. That's all part of His promise!

PRUNE OFF THE DEAD WOOD

Make a tree good and its fruit will be good, or make a tree bad and its fruit will be bad. For a tree is recognised by its fruit.

Matthew 12:33 NIV

The early spring is a time when we are encouraged to inspect our garden after the long cold winter. New buds emerge on bare branches ready to burst into fragrant blooms when the warmth of spring days arrive. Then, in preparation for the forthcoming summer, we set out to tidy our borders and clear away lifeless stems in order to promote new growth. We readily cut away anything that shows no evidence of life or producing new shoots. Eliminating those lifeless areas allows the plant to release its energy into the developing new buds on other stems. We can realise the benefits of discarding those parts which are no longer productive, yet so often with the 'dead wood' surrounding our personal issues we will be far less brutal than we are within our garden.

The fear of letting something go, even though it is clearly no longer good for us, often keeps us closer to it rather than allowing us freedom from it. Few things can be more daunting than the realisation that a long-term relationship has reached the end of the road, and it is time to take another path. Even when we do accept it, we can often lack the courage needed to make a complete break, and instead we might continue to keep in contact with the other person clutching at any threads that might hold the relationship together. Very often the one who finally makes the break will be overwhelmed with guilt at their decision, and any form of contact will help them to conceal it. In order to move forward and allow new growth in our lives we must be ready to cut off what is obviously no longer fruitful.

Pruning off the dead wood was one of the more difficult lessons

I learned after the initial separation from my first husband. I had dug up the root causes, dealt with many of the weeds and worms and then allowed my barriers to come crashing down. But I still needed to deal with the essential brutality of that final pruning and learn to let go of the things that were no longer a positive force for me.

It was my mum who encouraged me to cut back those areas and accept there were situations I needed to discard completely in order to move forward in my new life with Malc. Until then I had not considered how much my new growth was being stunted as I continued to have contact with my first husband and cling to those negative and lifeless areas of the life I had chosen to walk away from. We had a long history after all, and two teenage children who we both loved and had created many wonderful memories through the years of their growing. These bonds were what should have held us together, but alas, it was not enough of a reason to stay together. I needed to let go of all that was interfering with my new growth.

Unknowingly at the time, I had become completely stifled in my difficult marriage with Anthony, and even with a new reliable man in my life I was finding it impossible to completely let go of all that I was familiar with. Leaving Anthony had not given me automatic freedom from the past. My dependency on him was difficult to overcome because I did not have enough confidence to depend on myself let alone anyone else. His continuing efforts to manipulate me, even though we were living apart, only added to my fear that I might not be able to survive with the independence I desired. Such irrational thoughts clearly emphasised the severity of my mental state and how easy it was for Anthony to continue wearing me down.

I found it difficult to act on the advice that my family offered me even though most of the time I knew they were right. I actually had more strength than I gave myself credit for, and was not really as dependent on Anthony as I believed. He was a crutch that I was unaware I no longer needed. Remember as a child learning to ride your bike and feeling fully confident knowing that the back of the bike was being steadied by a grown-up? Then, after a while, you discovered that the grown-up had let go a while ago and you had been steering by yourself without knowing. Only once you had experienced the euphoria of balancing the bike unaided were you able to believe in yourself enough to go it alone.

Over the years, Anthony had stolen my confidence and convinced me I was not a likeable person and with that insecurity I continued to lean on him in a similar way to when I learned to ride my bike as a child. Malc could console me a million times and remind me I was a good person, but Anthony could strip me of any new confidence with just a few short words. For such a long time I had believed everything he told me about myself. I was fat, I was rude, and embarrassing. With my daughter's lean towards singing, karaoke was a popular night out for us all as a family. This gave my son a chance to hold the microphone for a while and sometimes they would both sing with their dad. I didn't have the confidence to get up and sing like the rest of my family, and Anthony often reminded me that I wasn't a very good singer, or he would tell me that I would make a fool of myself, and so I didn't even attempt to. When I did feel I was doing something well, he would need to be a part of it so that once again I didn't believe I had been able to make that accomplishment by myself. Each time he criticised me I allowed him to destroy my confidence further. Even after our separation I was still listening to him and believing most of what he said. Phone call after phone call I would be told that Malc was no good for me. He was too old and I would soon become bored and regret my decision. I am ashamed to admit that I did begin to question my decision. Maybe Malc was too old, and perhaps I did have my head in the clouds and would come crashing down at some point with a big thud! What if when that happened it was too late and Anthony didn't want me back? I was so afraid of being on my own that I questioned whether I was with Malc for the right reasons. I was becoming completely dependent on Anthony again, which was exactly what he wanted.

Since he had been the only man in my life for virtually all of my adult years, I struggled to imagine a situation of being totally separate from him. I had spent so many years under his control and was blinded from the very reasons that had driven me to leaving him. I spent long periods arguing with myself in my head over everything that had contributed to me having sunk to such low depths, but as soon as I imagined life without my 'crutch' I was afraid that I couldn't survive without it.

★ ★ ★

For some years after leaving my first husband, my daughter and I were unable to keep a functioning relationship without us becoming involved in a ferocious quarrel. In the end, the divorce had been even more traumatic and lengthy than I could have ever imagined and during that time I was aware that her father had exposed her to many ugly and untrue comments about me and details of the divorce. With his usual characteristic style, Anthony often managed to convince her that *he* was the injured party. Listening to his biased opinions instead of hearing both sides consequently led her into developing a great resentment towards me. At times I wished that she could have heard my side too, but rightly or wrongly I believed it was unfair to involve either of my children in a bitter war of 'tit for tat' between the two most influential people in their lives. Just as I remembered how my own father had never bad-mouthed my mother after they separated, so I believed I owed my children the same opportunity to work things out for themselves. I prayed hard that they would come to understand that not everything that Anthony told them was the truth, and that they would continue to love us equally as their parents without feeling a need to take sides.

In the depths of my psychological thinking I knew that my daughter loved me, but for a while she became caught in a world that was built on anger and resentment, which only seemed to make her thrive on angry outbursts with me. I had to be so careful how I approached her because the slightest of things could cause her to lose her temper with me. During this time she was also trying to cope with her own personal life-changing issues. She became pregnant with her then boyfriend, just six months after I left, which must have been an enormous thing for her to come to terms with by herself. Up until then, our relationship had always been open and I am certain that not having me around, particularly then, must have been overwhelming for her at times.

Though I tried to consider her own turmoil, her outbursts were sometimes vile as she screamed her aggression at me in bursts of inexcusable foul language. Consequently our relationship suffered severely and for a long time did not exist at all.

I hated the detachment between us in a way that I am unable to express and, just as I had done when my marriage had been in trouble, I used every logical instrument I could think of in an attempt to overcome the unreasonable outbursts but for some time nothing made a difference. The more I tried to reason and iron things out, the more it seemed that she delighted in knocking me down. In the early days friends would tell me that she would get over it in time and that it was natural for her to feel angry after her world had been turned upside down. I tried desperately to understand that, despite the vulgar scenes that often erupted when we were together. Not having her in my life was pain I had never known, and the prospect of us being severed indefinitely was something I could barely even think about.

During the first two years, I made many considerations to my own failing in our breakdown so as not to burden her with all the blame. Even though I felt completely destroyed, each time it came to the boil I would try to put the fight behind us and begin again as friends. However, my quick to forgive approach often left me open for another dose of fury from her when I didn't bend to her desires. It was a pattern that paralleled the one that I had encountered with her father and one that she was all too familiar with. As a child, her perception of me was as a person who was weak in character, afraid of confrontation and someone who usually gave in to ensure peace. In my new circumstances I had gained strength and, even though I still aimed for peace, I was beginning to learn that ensuring mutual harmony did not always mean having to give in to other people's demands. I suspect that like Anthony it may have been difficult for her to come to terms with this new strength, and I guess she assumed it would be easy to drag me down and meet her demands. For a while that was the case, and there were many times when both she and Anthony succeeded as my new strength began to sap and lose its impact. It would take some time for me to recharge my energy and continue to think for myself, but gradually I would bounce back enough to put myself back in control again.

I finally had to make the brave decision and prune the branches of the relationship with my daughter in the hope that they would later emerge with stronger shoots after a furious argument in my own home. Because of our differences, I found myself walking on eggshells most of the time when we were together. On one particular occasion when we had hardly seen each other in more than a year, she asked if she could come and visit me for a few days together with my son and my small grandson. I excitedly agreed and looked forward to spending time with my complete family. I enjoyed that unity very much, but after three days an obvious strain between my daughter and I emerged. I found myself needing to be deliberately careful of how I spoke and eventually the tension became too much. Without warning and from the most trivial matter, a violent, verbal argument broke out as she hurled spiteful threats at me. My son pleaded with her to be calm and rational but even her small toddler crying in the midst of the shouting did not stop her from her threatening and foul accusations towards me. In the end, with a heavy heart, I actually asked her to leave. After living with Malc for almost three years, I had moved on from such aggression, and I could not allow myself to be subjected to such attacks ever again. Momentarily, I realised that I did not have to accept those circumstances anymore and my decision to ask her to leave demonstrated a greater strength in me than I had ever known. After she drove away in her car, I took a look at my reflection in the mirror and through my sobbing breath I told myself that I would never tolerate a situation like that again. These outbursts had been happening for almost two years and I had made excuses for them in the same way that I had done with her father. For the first time ever I put myself first and found the strength to 'prune my shrub'.

My daughter was never to be dead wood in my life. The shoots would always grow back, and finally as her own life became more settled and content, the new growth appeared stronger than it was before. It took a great deal of pruning before that happened, but the relationship that developed between us from there became stronger. If there is still anger in her, I don't see it so often and it is no longer directed at me. I prayed so much that she would find contentment in her life and that she would eventually produce a spray of beautiful blooms again, like the ones I had seen in her before. My prayers for this were daily and there were times when I wondered if it was even in God's plans for us to have a functioning relationship. At one time I really doubted whether my prayers would be answered as the rift seemed to continue for so long. I could not allow my heart to be broken again, and I suspect that my daughter probably didn't know how to approach me. We were at stalemate. For a while we became stuck in a situation that neither of us were able to change, and we hardly spoke to each other at all. Both of us were a little stubborn, I guess, and I made a decision that I would not allow anyone to try to take control of me again. I can't describe the pain that this rift between us caused me, and I don't doubt for a second, that it was painful for her too. But I had discovered that love is built on kindness and trust, and all that is good. During that time, it was often difficult for me to see any of these things within our relationship, so I stepped back in the hope that in time, we would learn to be more understanding and offer each other the respect we both deserved. Then, one day after a church service and a particularly poignant prayer time, I contacted her and suggested we get together. By that time she was in a solid and loving relationship and I believe it was that which had freed her from much of her anger and frustrations. She had something wonderful to focus on and was enjoying all the rewards of a two-way, loving relationship. Today we are good friends and I am able to indulge in that friendship and enjoy the two beautiful grandchildren she has given me. I see how the Lord has planted in her the seeds from the Fruits of The Spirit which have encompassed her with a vine that bears much fruit and a purpose for her life.

★ ★ ★

It is not always possible to 'prune' with the assurance that things will grow back stronger. And sometimes stronger is not even what we believe we want. Often we would prefer things to be just as we are used to, rather than embracing something new and more positive. Fear of severing ourselves completely from what we are familiar with has the power to jeopardise our chances of progressing and, as with the shrubs in our garden, we often come across lifeless branches in our life that have no chance of growth. Pruning can leave things looking slightly off balance for a while, but a dead branch will only hinder the development of a neighbouring fruitful one. Our heartache at letting the original one go will eventually be swallowed up in the joy of the new shoots and the loveliness that they bring with them.

Waiting for new shoots to appear in the relationship with my daughter took longer than I could ever have imagined. It was unbearable as the rift between us also denied me the fulfilment of being close to her first child, my adorable grandson. Many people suggested I should give in for the sake of having him in my life, but I concluded that an obvious negative between me and his mummy would not create a positive force for him. In any case, if my daughter and I were ever to stand any chance of developing a strong relationship in the future, it had to be built on foundations of mutual respect and trust. Something that was unlikely to happen if we continued to fight as ferociously as we had in those earlier times.

★ ★ ★

As young people, most of us at one time or another have taken comforting advice from our friends and family as we have come to terms with the break up of another friend or our first love. "There are plenty more fish in the sea," we might have been told in an effort to console us. My dad would use a different phrase to overcome the same circumstances. "Where one door closes another one opens," he would optimistically tell me through my heartache or disappointment when some young boy broke my heart. Spiritually I have learned how right he was. Each episode of our life has a purpose and God never closes one door without another one being readily available to us. This understanding has helped me to accept that God is present in all suffering, and that each painful experience has a purpose. It is not always obvious to us at the time, and God may only reveal His intentions in the aftermath. Through the consequences of my own experiences, I have gained an inner strength which is far greater than I could ever have imagined. God has been a guide through all my situations, and His gentle, spiritual nurturing has provided me with everything I need to overcome any circumstances. Whatever our beliefs, and even for those who do not yet experience the joy of a faithful relationship with God, we can't expect to experience the rewards of beautiful foliage unless we are prepared to regularly nurture it and trim away any dead wood.

It took a huge amount of time to make progress in my relationship with my daughter, and of course not everything that went wrong between us was her fault. She was experiencing her own pressures as she took on being a single mum after the break up with her son's father. She was, I am sure, completely devastated by her own parents break up, and added to that I didn't always approach things in the most sensitive way as I dealt with my own frustrations at trying to come to terms with the rift between us.

On the other side of my shrub however, there was pruning to be done that was clearly dead wood. When I was finally brave enough to cut my first husband off completely, two significant things happened. Eventually, he tired of contacting me with vicious and threatening text messages or calls that no longer upset me, but more importantly I was able to move forward with new confidence and a realisation that I no longer needed my 'crutch' and I was able to walk freely. An independent person emerged from what had once been little more than a shrinking violet and, in the same way that I had prayed for the seeds from the Fruits of the Spirit for my daughter, I too, discovered the delights of love, joy, peace, patience, kindness, goodness, faithfulness, gentleness and self control. (Galatians 5:22)

BIN BAGS OR COMPOST?

It is fit neither for the soil, nor for the manure heap; it is thrown out.
Luke 14v35 NIV

As I began the preparation for writing this chapter, I was at times overwhelmed as I reflected on the enormous amount of debris that had been left behind once my wall had fallen and the dead wood had been pruned. As I attempted to clear the path, the weight of the rubble sometimes seemed too heavy for me to shift. What little emotional strength I still had at the end of my first marriage had been sapped during its demolition, and my energies became lost among the debris and dust which gathered around me.

The troubled mind often struggles to make considerations in a rational manor. Instead, it prefers to cling to things that the logically thinking mind would joyfully release. Guilt hangs heavily, as does fear. The two fit perfectly hand in hand.

Despite a new contented life with Malc in a home and job that I loved, I was still heavily burdened by an inner critic who insisted on dragging me down at a time when I should have been consumed with feelings of elation and excitement about the future. However, the new mind games that Anthony played once I left him only added to my confusion, and the guilty feelings that had been familiar to me throughout our marriage flooded my head more than ever. I felt responsible for just about everything, and at rock bottom neither of my children spoke to me. In my heart I knew that was not my fault, but I felt guilty that I had left them and was no longer a part of their everyday life. To justify my guilt I looked for as many reasons as I could to burden myself instead of accepting that I was not responsible for everything that had happened and that the decisions I had made had been to preserve my sanity.

Malc dealt with these sensitive issues as delicately as he knew how, but, often because he was at the very core of it, I found it impossible to be open with him about my deepest feelings. Instead, I would respond with angry outbursts because his opinion was "not what I wanted to hear". I confided in my parents and closest friends and, though their advice was usually parallel to Malc's, I never displayed my frustration towards them in the same way as I did him. He was intensely patient as he held my hand and walked with me over each and every broken stone that covered the path before me. As desperation crept up on me, I turned to my Bible in an effort to verify the advice of my loved ones. God fast became my friend as I realised I could talk to Him in confidence and without judgement. Then, for the first time, I saw things in the Bible that I had not discovered before.

The Holy Bible is a powerful self-help book. Its pages are filled with inspirational stories of characters who endured similar dilemmas to those that so many of us face at one time or another. Such a realisation became a huge reassurance to me as I learned to understand that I was not isolated or unique. Every situation we can ever imagine can be clarified within the pages of this Holy Book. During those initial months when I was desperate for answers and encouragement I drew much strength from its content. Primarily, I realised that Jesus Himself had endured every trouble that I was still struggling to deal with. He is able to affiliate with anything we share with Him because He has first-hand experience of *all* our situations. This is confirmed throughout much of the New Testament.

The story of Mary and Lazarus in John 11 highlights His human emotions when Jesus is told that Lazarus, His friend, has died. The shortest, and possibly one of the most powerful verses in the Bible reads, 'Jesus wept.' (John 11:35) clearly demonstrates to us that as powerful as He was as the Son of God, He was equally as humble as the rest of us, having to overcome emotions that ran high and situations that hurt Him intensely. By the time I had read the Gospels thoroughly for the first time in my life, I knew I could put my trust in Him, because there was nothing that had happened in my life that He had not experienced Himself. At times He had been outcast by His own friends and the people He trusted. He had been tempted by sin and lost friends when He stood by all that He believed in. He was a human who had experienced emotions and disappointments in all the same ways that we do. There was nothing I could take to Him that He would not understand. This was a great comfort.

* * *

With my mental anguish consuming me as I attempted to clear away the rubble as well as deal with all the weeds and the worms, I spoke to my minister. Explaining some of the background issues to him for the first time as well as the heart-wrenching ones over the relationship with my daughter, I used the familiar term that many of us use to describe such a heavy load. Baggage. I explained that I was aware that the 'emotional baggage' I carried often marred the otherwise stable and contented life I shared with Malc. He listened and allowed me to pour out all that I needed to release with gentle sensitivity before he offered his advice.

"When you use the term 'baggage' in the way that you do," he began, "what you are suggesting is that, like real baggage, your troubles are laying heavily on you and are a huge burden. If you imagine that you are carrying a loaded rucksack with you wherever you go, then at some point on your journey it will weigh you down and slow your pace. Your journey will continue but the weight of your load will bear a heavy yoke and your energies will be drained. In order to make that journey more comfortable you will need to put the baggage down and leave it. Only when you do that will you experience the sense of freedom that will allow you to continue on your way." His words were greatly encouraging and I understood his theory. I needed to learn how to release myself from the unnecessary guilt and anguish I was carrying in order to move forward freely.

I considered the scenario of a traveller with a heavy load on his back, and for the following few days I tossed over and over in my mind the encouraging advice from my minister. I knew that offloading in such a way would not come easily. Anthony had created a great deal of the 'baggage', but much of it centred on my daughter and I could not contemplate continuing my journey without her. The baggage I was carrying was unlike the 'dead wood' I had recently pruned. My load was the guilt that had made a home with me over a number of years. Much of that guilt had manifested more recently over the severity of the relationship between myself and my daughter. As well as the guilt, I was also weighed down with my memories, both good and bad, of everything that my first marriage had been. It was incredibly hard for me to put the bag down and continue my journey without it.

Never could I contemplate letting go of my beautiful daughter, which was what I was most afraid of. I tossed this frightening scenario over and over in my mind wondering how on earth I could free myself of my 'baggage' and still have her with me as I moved onwards. It then occurred to me one day that once all the ground work is complete, when the weeds and the worms are under control, the wall is demolished and all dead wood removed, we should then consider whether any of what is left may have a purpose for the future. Some situations need to be properly pruned and discarded as they serve no meaningful purpose in our lives. However, others can prove to be valuable lessons that will provide a good grounding for us later, in a similar way to our recycling methods on the compost heap.

Whilst it is healthy to make ourselves answerable for the mistakes we are genuinely responsible for, we need to face accountability rationally and accept that genuine mistakes can provide valuable lessons, which are all part of a healthy maturing that we can gain greatly from. Such learning will create invaluable richness within our own personal soil. Continually carrying those wrongs around as unnecessary burdens can eat away and damage the soul.

As a Christian I have learned how Jesus doesn't expect us to carry the weight of our errors and burdens with us. While we should be accountable for our own mistakes, we should not be weighed down with worthless worries that do not belong to us. Once we acknowledge that we have made wrong decisions or unjust actions Jesus allows us to leave them with Him at the foot of the cross. All we have to do is to genuinely repent from our wrongs. To understand what it means to genuinely repent, we simply have to accept from within the pit of our conscience that we have been wrong, hand it to Jesus, and the Holy Spirit will grant us freedom from all that has gone before. By releasing ourselves from our burdens and using our experiences as valuable fodder for our compost heap, we can prepare a nourishing stimulant for future situations when they need a positive direction.

★ ★ ★

During the initial months that Malc and I were together, my troubled state of mind had not only been a consequence of the lengthy controlled relationship I had endured throughout my first marriage, but was also the direct result of the cunning mind games Anthony played with me after I had left him. As his attempts to lure me back to him failed, he needed to contrive other ideas to attack my conscience and lower my morale further. In the past he had known exactly how to engineer that and my new outward strength was a huge blow to that capability. Very quickly he had to learn to play an even harder game. Then, one by one, he could introduce new fears into me in the hope of gaining back some of his power.

For a while, I am sure, Anthony thought of me as his trophy, one that he considered he was entitled to since it had already belonged to him for almost twenty years. In a desperate effort to hold on to it he reverted to any strategy that would ensure him of that possession. When the gentle approach failed he used a different tactic by threatening me and creating as much fear as possible hoping to make me desperate and needy once again.

Within a six month, period and at a time when I was still fragile, he subjected me to the most horrendous ordeals by using every emotional blackmail plot he could devise. As each attempt failed to bring him what he wanted, he had to think on his feet and be prepared with yet another. One day when he was no further forward in claiming back his prize, he played his trump card.

Living away from my children was the toughest thing that I ever had to deal with on a day-to-day basis. Anthony was very much aware of that. I had always been a good mother and that could not be denied. Since the break up I had regularly driven the three hundred mile round trip to be with them every ten days or whenever there was a particular need for me to be with them. One morning he phoned me and said he needed to talk. The conversation began amicably and he explained that he had finally understood that I had moved on and was unlikely to go back to him. It was a refreshing change from the recent hostility between us to be able to converse with him in that way and, in a moment of weakness and false confidence, I let down my guard as I enjoyed a civil moment with him.

As the conversation continued, his voice dropped and he seemed sad and hurt. With my guard down I felt sorry for his pain and felt a need to console him. He said that since he realised I was unlikely to go back to him he needed to make plans to move forward with his own life. I was somewhat uplifted to finally hear him acknowledge the inevitable, but also sad to admit that this was finally the very end of our relationship. He continued to speak in a low tone and told me how he could not face living in our home without me because the memories were too painful for him. For the same reason he also felt that he could no longer be around our mutual friends in social situations. All in all he had decided there was nothing left for him where he was and, having discussed it at length with our children the three of them had decided to emigrate to Canada to live near his sister. This news was more shattering than I can begin to explain as I considered the impracticality of trying to maintain a functioning relationship with my children with more than three thousand miles between us.

During the next few weeks I lived on the edge as I considered this impossible scenario. Malc and I argued non-stop as he tried to get me to think rationally. He was able to see through Anthony's empty threat but I was too afraid to take any chances on its reality and have my children living on the other side of the world. Anthony called me many times in the next couple of weeks reminding me of their plans and how excited they were by them. The children also shared their excitement and eventually I cracked under the pressure and concluded that a new beginning might be the answer for all four of us. I considered that if we all went to Canada we could overcome everything that had gone before and start all over again. The life I had shared with Malc in just a few short months was almost idyllic. He was stable in every way and his love for me was unquestionable. I had never known love such as that which I had shared with him. Therefore, it was ridiculous to convince myself that with a new start in a new country I could create some of what I had discovered with Malc with the only other man I had known and loved as an adult. But that was exactly what I did.

Malc and I argued more and more and most of those arguments were instigated by me as I used them to cover my guilt while I contemplated leaving this wonderful man and returning to the one I had fought so hard to escape from. Eventually, after causing yet another argument, I cowardly left Malc a note one morning while he was at work. Before I was even halfway along the motorway I realised my terrible mistake. Torn between promising to return to the man I knew or staying with the one I wanted to be with, I reacted like a frightened rabbit on the roadside. Terrified by the headlights in front of me and with eyes darting in every direction, I was unable to make an accurate judgment. I had made my rash decision only out of fear of losing my children, not for any other reason.

I cannot be sure whether it was at that point that I realised I no longer loved Anthony or whether that was when I discovered how much I loved Malc. Nonetheless, I knew almost immediately that I could not move back to the house I had shared with Anthony for so many years. Still blinded by the full beam of the headlights, I was more afraid and confused than ever. Having built up my children's confidence that I was about to move back with them, I was unable to find the courage to tell them I had made a massive mistake. Unable to be honest with them and refusing to move back into the house with Anthony, I made the ridiculous decision to live in my car, and, for the following nine weeks, that was more or less what I did. I was fortunate to have the offer of a bed most nights through my circle of friends, but I spent my days driving around my small hometown or spending time with my children in my old home while Anthony was at work. I refused to unpack my things and so everything I owned remained stacked in the back of my faithful old Renault Five!

Malc hurt so much for what I did, and I didn't deserve him to stand by me, but despite the cowardly way I had left him, he still chose not to desert me. With his outer vision he could see the dreadful mistake I would have made if I had moved back to my marital home. Once again I had made an irrational decision only through fear and he could see that. He kept in regular contact throughout this terrible time, and despite his own frustrations he waited with immense patience for me to work things out and find the courage to tell Anthony for a second time that I was leaving him. As Anthony worked out for himself that he was losing another round, it wasn't long before he worked out his next scheme. Going to Canada had never been a serious consideration, and I discovered that very quickly. Early one morning while staying at a friend's house, I took a disturbing call from my daughter. The panic in her voice was noticeable immediately.

"What did you say to Dad yesterday?" she asked me in an anxious and accusing tone.

"Nothing that I haven't said to him before. Just that I don't think I am going to go back to him, but I've been trying to say that for some time. Why, what's the matter?" I asked, feeling uneasy by her panic.

"Well he just came in my room before he went to work and kissed me goodbye, but he seemed very odd when he left, so I followed him to his car but when he saw me he locked the doors and drove off. I'm really scared Mum, I really feel as if he isn't coming back. I've tried to call him, but he won't answer his mobile." She continued talking very quickly and I too sensed that something was very wrong.

At first I was baffled by her jumbled words but concerned that she may have had a valid reason to be fearful, so I suggested that she and her brother made their way to where I was staying with my friend. By the time they arrived she had received a text message from her dad, which read: "I have told your mother that I cannot live without her and I can't. When she opens her car she will find a note." Very quickly I realised that the note was one I would not want to read so I called the police. My suspicions were right. He had written a seven page letter of both love and hate explaining that he had decided to take his life. We all tried relentlessly to call his mobile phone but though it was switched on, he wouldn't answer. The police were very thorough in their questioning and since I did not have enough courage to read the letter myself, they read it for me. They suggested it was best that I did not see the content, since it was filled with disturbing threats and anger directed at me together with a declaration of his unfailing love. As the hours passed and there was no word from him, I found myself in a surreal situation as I considered that he may well have done some harm to himself.

The next six hours seemed like days as the three of us tried constantly to get him to answer his phone without success. None of his friends had seen or heard from him, and for a while I really did fear the worst. The police had to break into his office to see if there was anything there that might give us some ideas, but nothing helped. When they asked if I could give them a description of any distinguishing marks such as tattoos my son eagerly chipped in that he had some on his arms. I knew that he thought that would be helpful in case he should be seen walking though a shopping centre or some other public place. But my heart sank as I realised that these were for identification purposes, in case they found his body. I was so angry at that moment as I watched the desperation in my son's face, as he worried for his dad. All we could do was to wait either for him to contact us, or to take that dreaded call from the police. With no rationality to my thinking, I momentarily considered that if he had taken his life I would finally be free from his clutches and in that brief moment I felt released, even euphoric. However, alongside that, I was consumed with the dread that my children would blame me and hold me responsible for his selfish actions. That fear overrode any of the irrational feelings of relief.

Finally, late into the afternoon, he called my daughter and eventually after much persuading he spoke to me and told me where he was. The whole thing had never been about him taking his life, it was his next attempt to bring him maximum sympathy in the hope that it would make me change my mind and stay with him. The fact that his own children had suffered such torment appeared irrelevant as he carried out this newest exercise to tug on my guilt strings once again.

The 'suicide' plot was a massive obstacle for me to overcome as I attempted to straighten out my head, but eventually I found the courage to go back and pick up my relationship with Malc. Anthony's war was still not over though, and a few weeks later I received the first of several phone calls from a woman claiming to be his friend. In our twenty years together I had no recollection of this woman but nonetheless I initially took her at face value. Within a few minutes I realised that she was not who she seemed as she calculatingly accused me of being a bad mother and a heartless bitch who had broken my husband's heart.

"Do you know what you're doing to him?" she asked venomously. "You've destroyed him and your children hate you for it."

I was completely traumatized by her spiteful accusations. I had no idea who this woman was, I didn't recognise her voice, and I had never known Anthony to have a friend by the name she gave me. But I was quick on my feet to know that I could not allow her to realise that she had affected me so badly. Sarcastically and in an act only of bravado, I thanked her for her observations and suggested that she continued to look out for Anthony since they were obviously such close friends. Anthony flatly denied knowing anyone by the name she had given and on that occasion I believed that he had no prior knowledge of the phone call. The second call came exactly a week later with the same accusing tone as before. Once again Anthony refused to acknowledge knowing the caller and for a couple of months I heard no more from her.

Just when I had put the calls behind me, Malc received another one from her. In the depths of my heart I knew that Anthony was behind them. However, as he profusely denied knowing anything about them I chose to believe that even he could not stoop low enough to inflict such maliciousness on me. I was greatly disturbed each time she called, and Anthony's sympathy deflected my suspicions away from him, intensifying my anguish as I tried to discover who else might be behind them.

The next time she called, Anthony told me that he believed it was our daughter. It was true that at that time we were struggling to get along and she had an obvious dislike for Malc, which Anthony suggested gave her a valid reason to upset us. She was eighteen at the time and, for all of her faults, I never believed that she could have instigated such vicious attacks on me. The telephone conversations were always aimed at building sympathy for Anthony and hard as it was to accept, I realised that the only person who could truly be behind them other than the caller was him.

Eventually the caller became brave enough to call our house and speak to Malc. She coldly told him that I constantly lied to him, and that I was planning to go back to Anthony again. Furious and frustrated at this latest intrusion, I called Anthony and suggested that he must surely know who she was. What I neglected to tell him was that this time she had called us at home.

In the midst of those distressing calls, Anthony had also fabricated a cancer scare by informing me that he had discovered two lumps in his testicles. I was understandably concerned to hear this and encouraged him to seek medical help straight away. The 'results' came back clear, but even before I got home to Malc that same day, our mystery caller had already advised him what a lucky man he was and that had Anthony been diagnosed with cancer I had planned to go back to him. It was evident at that point that Anthony was the one behind the calls but I still had no proof.

Several months later, while we were discussing an issue over my son's schooling, the conversation diverted to the phone calls and Anthony mentioned the time when the woman had called us at home. Knowing I had never told him that she had called our home, I was able to conclude without any doubt that he had instigated those calls which had subjected me to the most blatant spitefulness I had ever known. He had set the whole thing up to cause me maximum distress and hopefully cause a rift between me and Malc. On realising he was beaten, he was still not prepared to stay down and then made up the most outrageous story to clear his name and make Malc the villain! He relayed an unbelievable story to both me and my daughter, with so many loopholes that it made no sense. However, my daughter was convinced by her dad and would not listen to the clear and valid reasons that proved Malc could never have been involved. We never heard from the woman again after I exposed Anthony, but the damage to the relationship between me and my daughter was severe and long term.

Anthony's ridiculous claims led me to conclude that the time had come to draw up divorce papers and make my final move forward. That process took almost four years as he continually dragged his feet in an effort to cause as much disruption as he could get away with for as long as possible.

When I look back to some of those unbearable situations, there is as much for me to draw strength from as there is to discard completely. Anthony's attempt to lure me back with a false emigration threat and then leaving us to wonder whether he was dead or alive took me to the lowest places I have ever been to. Together with those alarming phone calls and a fabricated cancer scare, I often questioned my sanity. These types of situations are not normal to me and I cannot thrive in such turmoil. The hole that I sank into was dark and frightening, but once I found the courage to climb out of it, I discovered strength and vitality inside of me that I may otherwise have never known. I no longer dwell on those circumstances, they are far behind me. I have discarded what is no longer needed and used the lessons I have learned from them as fertiliser to feed my soul.

★ ★ ★

When the Bible was new to me there were times when I was puzzled that Jesus made friends with people you might least expect Him to. Mary Magdalene had been a common prostitute in her time. Jesus did not judge her by her past, instead He loved her for who she became; His loyal friend. We know also that He shared supper with tax collectors and was an open friend to Lazarus, who was an outcast of the people. Through these surprising relationships, He has taught us that, despite our past, each of us are equal and can be released from all that has gone before if we are ready to repent and follow Him.

My parish vicar reminded me of these stories when we spoke about my own 'baggage'. Guilt and repentance work side by side. You cannot feel guilty about your actions unless you are genuinely sorry for them. And if you are truly sorry for your failings, Jesus forgives you. With that freedom it is not necessary for us to carry the burdens of guilt around with us in heavy rucksacks that weigh us down. Instead, we should try to establish what needs to be emptied into bin bags and discarded and what we can use to throw on the compost and enrich us in the future.

I have thrown all sorts of rubbish into the compost bin in my garden. It all looks worthless as it goes in, but over time as it ferments and breaks down it changes form completely and becomes the most nourishing fodder to use on the garden. Life experiences have the same potential, and just as it is not useful to throw everything onto the compost, we must decide which of our experiences have been valuable lessons, and which are weighing us down and are best to be completely discarded.

THE BIRDS AND THE BEES

The husband should fulfil his marital duty to his wife,
and likewise the wife to her husband.
1 Corinthians 7:3 NIV

This chapter deals with the most delicate and intimate matters I needed to come to terms with as I rebuilt my broken confidence. As I prepared to write it, I was conscious that I needed to consider these personal issues with great care and be certain in my mind that I could cover them sensitively. I did not include it to draw sympathy towards myself or to direct unnecessary accusations against my first husband. Though I suffered much naivety at the time, I do realise now that the physical bond between a man and woman is perfectly natural and should be a wonderful way to express such mutual love. The Bible tells us clearly from the very beginning, in the book of Genesis, that God understood that Adam needed a companion to share his life with. Regularly, throughout the Old and the New Testament, we are reminded of that very special gift of intimate love that God wants us to indulge in.

The subject of intimate problems within a partnership can be the most difficult to talk about or to come to terms with. The very idea of discussing with one another our concerns over such a subject can be a little embarrassing even in the closest of relationships. Added to that we can also hold back if we become fearful of hurting the other party, who we love deeply, by suggesting to them that things are not quite the way we would like them to be. Even in today's modern and open society some people still find discussing their sexual desires a bit of a taboo area, and, sadly, where such concerns are not addressed sensitively at the time, the problem can widen and can even be the underlying reason that a relationship fails. However, a functioning physical relationship is a basic, fundamental ingredient in the relationship between a husband and wife. Therefore, it is absolutely essential that each party should feel relaxed and fulfilled in that way.

Sitting in my garden one summer afternoon and organising my thoughts as I prepared how I would write this chapter, I was distracted by a bumble bee buzzing around the flowerpots on my patio. Every now and again the buzzing stopped as he nuzzled himself deep into the heart of a flower head and collected pollen. He seemed to busy himself for quite some time before hopping onto a neighbouring flower, repeating his nuzzling and then flying away again into the warm air. That part of his job was complete and he could take his collection of pollen back to his hive.

At the other end of the garden in the shallow water of my bird bath and shaded from the heat of the sun by the full leaves of a lilac tree, I also watched two sparrows cool themselves from the heat of the summer sun. It was mesmerising to watch them fluttering their wings as they hopped playfully in and out of the water. Summer is such a joyful season, especially in the garden. The flowers are in their fullness and are nourished by the lazy warmth of the sun as well as the welcome watering of a cool shower.

In my thoughts I considered how the animal kingdom differs widely to that of mankind. Animals normally mate in seasons or on impulse alone. Emotional attachment is rare among wildlife. In most species heartache is unapparent, as is commitment. In Genesis, we learn that when God made mankind He put us above all other living creatures, setting us aside from the rest. It was His intention for man and woman to engage in faithful relationships that would be filled with love, respect and kindness as well as intimacy. Our bodies were designed to desire one another and to fulfil that need within the boundaries of a loving committed relationship.

During puberty, our bodies begin to prepare for meeting these physical needs. Our hormones change dramatically, often creating different mood swings along with the need to explore our sexuality. The onset of a relationship is often passionately charged and exciting, however, over time, that charge tends to subside and a new pattern of loving takes over. The intensity is replaced with an intimacy that is considerate to the needs of our partner, and common interests or standards become a different form of attraction to us in that person. The need to share physical love with each other changes from a longing to draw pleasure for ourselves into one of giving pleasure back to each other. No other living creature shares desires in quite the same intense way. Physical attraction and desire is a natural gift that God granted to us from the very beginning (Genesis 2:24). There is no shame in these needs as this physical contentment is a vital communication within a loving relationship.

⋆ ⋆ ⋆

Anthony and I greatly lacked intimacy throughout most of our relationship and this void absolutely aided the downfall of our marriage. In the beginning, when we were young and first married, we enjoyed regular physical intimacy together. Slowly, over time and particularly after the birth of our children, many things prevented us from sharing such a special time with each other. Like many new mothers I became increasingly tired while I tended to the needs of my young children. My day was usually exhausting looking after them mainly on my own, and my bed was often a place of great comfort and one where I could relax and wind down from my hectic day. I would regularly suggest that Anthony and I go to bed at the same time, not necessarily to make love each time, but also so that we could enjoy the intimacy of being alone and uninterrupted by the children. Many times I would have been content to be curled up in his arms, but his usual response was that he was not properly relaxed unless he had watched TV for a good part of the evening. I was never as interested in the TV as Anthony, but I often attempted to stay up later just so I could be with him. However, as the evening drew on I would have to give in and crawl into my bed alone. A pattern began to unfold, and it became quite normal for us to almost always go to bed at different times. Often I would wake up in the small hours and slip down the stairs to find him fast asleep with the TV still on and the remains of a half eaten takeaway on the floor beside him. Like everything else, I made many excuses for this and was always thankful when he finally crawled into bed beside me.

As the years moved on he became more and more drawn towards late night TV, and I began to feel desperately neglected and unloved. I questioned myself because my husband seemed uninterested in lying next to me, and my confidence took another slide. On the rare occasions that I managed to persuade him to come to bed at the same time as me he was usually accompanied by a video together with crisps, chocolate and a bottle of cola! It is somewhat outrageous as I recall this time, that I allowed him to continue this behaviour, but I had become so timid over the years for fear of upsetting him and sending him to a rage, that I seldom questioned anything that he did. My desires to be intimate would shatter as I was subjected to watching a film that did not interest me as well as listening to his regular munching. I was forced to resign myself that wanting to tenderly finish our day together was not what Anthony wanted. The closeness I longed for was not important to him so I began to allow him to sleep on the sofa undisturbed. I would sometimes go and wake him up in the small hours and sometimes I just left him. Many times he would crawl into bed shortly before my alarm went off to get the children up for school.

When we were first married, I was a young and naive twenty-one year old with virtually no sexual experience. Over the years as I matured into womanhood, my body cried out for an intimate affection that Anthony had no desire to share with me. Then as my hunger for physical love continued to be unfulfilled, I became convinced that such desires were unreasonable and I was placing too much pressure on him. Anthony would only emphasise this point by telling me constantly that being married was not just about sex, and that it was far more important to have friendship within a marriage. At the time, I believed that we were great friends, and since I worried that my growing desires were unreasonable I stopped making physical demands on him and mostly waited silently, hoping that he would approach me. This silent anticipation could continue for several months and that physical lust was usually only fulfilled two or three times in any one year. When it did happen, it was selfish and unrewarding for either of us as we both drew from it our own needs without thinking about each other in the selfless act of loving that I have since discovered.

The woman I am now finds it astonishing that I could have accepted being so neglected. It emphasises yet again how low I had sunk during that time as I concluded that every rejection was a failing in myself rather than realise how unreasonable and self centred my husband was. Having no real understanding that Anthony was also manipulating our sex life, I once again consumed myself with guilt.

In desperation to come to terms with my 'unreasonable' desires, I finally broke my silence and confided in a close friend and explained to her how much I longed just to be touched and that I often fantasised about experiencing sexual fulfilment with my husband. When I explained that in any one year we would make love no more than two or three times she was truly astounded. Nonetheless, it was true that many months would easily pass without any physical contact between us at all, not even a tender goodnight kiss in each other's arms. I began to make a mental diary of how long would pass without us even touching each other tenderly in our bed, and many times it would be more than eight months. Then when it did happen I would usually feel immediately disappointed that I would almost certainly have to wait a long time before I would manage to have his attention in that way again. When I tried to instigate things between us he would sometimes use the excuse that he had a low sex drive and would push me away. Or else he would focus his stony face onto whatever he was watching on the television and ignore my attempts to arouse him. In hindsight, I should have questioned whether he was having an affair, but at that time it truly never crossed my mind. Despite my sexual frustration, I could never have contemplated being with another man and it never occurred to me that he would want to be with anyone else either. We were good friends (or so I believed) and had a mutual love for our children, and at that time I believed that was enough to keep our marriage together.

Many years later I discovered that Anthony did have a brief relationship with a close, mutual friend. It was something he was never willing to own up to while we were together, and he only finally admitted it to me after I had left him. My heart told me it was happening, and most women would have confronted such a situation, but I was again afraid of the consequences. My greatest fear always was that he would leave me. The idea of being alone was something I could not contemplate because I had become completely dependent on him. When I first suspected the affair, the only way I felt comfortable enough to raise the issue was to delicately suggest that our 'friend' seemed to be spending more time with him than was perhaps healthy. I suggested that she had designs on him even if he didn't realise it. By taking this approach, I placed the emphasis on her rather than him and tried not to sound as though I were accusing either of them. His reaction was in keeping with his normal character. He became volatile and defensive. In his anger he twisted my gentle suggestion to such a point that I regretted ever having raised the subject. He was so defensive that he convinced me that I had imagined it all. In his angry state at being questioned, he told me that I had "lost the plot," and suggested that I seek counselling. This suggestion was anger loaded rather than a way to help our situation. There was nothing wrong with my mental health and he was aware of that, but once again I questioned myself and readily loaded up my rucksack with even more guilt.

The insecurities I acquired over Anthony's affair caused me to become more and more frustrated by his physical rejections. He insisted I had no reason to suspect foul play and because of that I felt guilt loaded and my conscience forced me to do all that I could to make up to our 'friend' for even thinking she might have had designs on my husband. I ridiculously went out of my way to make her my best friend and over time I stupidly shared with her some of my most intimate concerns about my relationship. Her willingness to listen empathetically was a huge comfort to me and when she reassured me that I had been wrong about her and Anthony, her forgiveness was a tremendous relief.

Anthony on the other hand did little to reassure me that I was the one he loved and wanted, and with continued rejections I finally plucked up the courage to speak to him one Sunday morning when I thought we were both relaxed and had time on our hands. As I waited patiently for him to stir from his sleep, I considered how I would delicately approach him and explain how lonely I had become. I felt more lonely when he was actually in the bed than when I was there on my own and he was sleeping in front of the TV. Almost as if his instincts gave him forewarning that I wanted to talk, he jumped out of bed as soon as he opened his eyes and went downstairs without saying a word, leaving me crying into my pillow.

After a while he became irritated by my sobs and flew back into the bedroom in a furious rage. "I can't cope with this crap," he bellowed at me as I quivered at his brutality. "What the f*** is wrong with you now?" Through pathetic sobs I told him how desperately lonely I was and that I just wanted to feel loved and fulfilled. It was the first time I had ever challenged him so openly, and instantly his temper sobered and he flopped gently on to the bed beside me. With his head in his hands he softly told me that he was experiencing a 'problem'.

"I'm impotent," he whispered, looking at me pitifully. "I want to love you, but I can't do that stuff at the moment."

This revelation was shocking and something I had not expected to hear. It instantly broke my heart as I considered how the man I loved had been suffering by himself while all the time I had been putting him under further pressure by making demands on him that he was physically unable to fulfil. I reached out and cradled him in my arms, gently reassuring him it was not a situation he needed to deal with alone. From now on we would work through it together.

We talked for some time and I felt enormous sadness for my husband, while at the same time I found I was excited at the prospect of rediscovering each other as we went about overcoming what I believed was a manageable hurdle in our marriage. I saw it as a wonderful opportunity to fulfil many of my long-felt fantasies by finding new and exciting ways to bring pleasure to each other without the need for him to be pressured into having to perform full intercourse.

My first suggestion was that we discuss it together with our doctor but he was adamant that it was something he wanted to deal with on his own, and because I feared breaking the incredible closeness I was experiencing at that moment, I agreed. For the rest of that day I felt more bonded with him than as long as I could remember. I was completely lifted believing that Anthony's lack of interest in me was not personal and, despite it being a situation I had not been expecting to discover, I also anticipated the prospect of a new exciting beginning for us both.

Several weeks passed and though neither of us mentioned the 'problem', I felt close and protective towards him. I was tender but conscious not to touch him in a provocative way for fear of him feeling pressured. I had been sexually frustrated for many years but all that frustration had dispersed because I believed my husband needed me as well as the reassurance that I loved him. Throughout our whole marriage I was the one who had felt needy and insecure, but now for the first time I was able to offer as much reassurance as necessary to restore any insecurities his 'problem' might have caused him. We snuggled together on the sofa most evenings, which was something we had not done for several years. We kissed and caressed and there was no pressure on him because I was happy indulging in the gentle intimacy of togetherness. It was a beautiful time for me as I anticipated his healing. In the back of my mind I was never sure how that healing would come about but I was afraid to raise the subject for fear of breaking the magical spell between us. I assumed that time was all that was needed for him to regain his confidence and then we would begin to make love together in a way neither of us had ever experienced before. It was an opportunity for me to consider all my fantasies guilt free! We continued to go to bed at different times, but I no longer felt neglected when he wasn't beside me. In time, I was sure that everything would change.

Then one night a couple of months later, I felt him slip into bed in the small hours and I was aware that he had switched on the TV. While he assumed I was still sleeping I discovered that he was watching an 'X' rated film with the sound switched off. After a few minutes I was aware that he was masturbating as he lay beside me. I felt tense and uncomfortable at this realisation but continued to lay with my back to him pretending to be asleep. I was afraid of embarrassing him if he discovered that I was awake. Once his urge had been satisfied, he flicked off the TV and went to sleep. I never mentioned what had happened partly to spare his own embarrassment, but equally as much to spare mine. I was that naïve that I actually believed his self pleasure was aiding his recovery. On two further occasions I became even more confused as I was subjected to the motions in my bed for several minutes as he satisfied himself. I would lie with my back to him, rigid with fear while I waited for it to finish. I can't be sure what I was afraid of, I just know I hated every second of it. In the end, whether I believed it was helping him or not the situation became too uncomfortable and upsetting. My embarrassment was replaced by fear as I anticipated a violent outburst if he ever discovered that I was aware of what he was doing. I arranged for the VCR to be moved into our son's bedroom, and once it was set it up there Anthony never masturbated in our bed again. What he did in front of the TV downstairs I will never know, but I was no longer subjected to his demeaning actions.

Ridiculous as it sounds, being forty years old, and, in spite of these late night sessions, I honestly was so inexperienced, that I didn't understand what had really been happening in my bed. I still believed that he was impotent, and honestly thought that the 'X' rated films were helping him to overcome the problem. Since we had never discussed whether he was getting better or not and I was afraid to mention it to him, I went to see my doctor in the hope that he could advise me on how I could help to encourage Anthony through his recovery. Because of my naivety at that time, I really didn't understand that it is not possible for a man to masturbate if he is impotent! It was incredibly humiliating when my doctor explained to me that by going through that process, there was actually nothing physically wrong with him, and that maybe we should consider relationship counselling to help us improve communication within our relationship. This revelation hit me very hard, because at that point I was still not fully aware of just how far our marriage had been sliding. However, as the lies that he had exposed me to in order that he could cover up his own failings when he had found me crying in my bed that morning were revealed to me for the first time, it was clear that we did indeed need outside help if our marriage was going to survive.

By challenging him that morning I had pushed him into a corner, and rather than discuss my feelings with me and accept some responsibility, he chose to make himself the victim, and therefore gained all the attention that I had been craving from him. This cruel and humiliating deception that he had kept up for months while I had done everything I could to be a loving wife and take all pressure away from him struck home as I understood that after almost twenty years of giving all of myself, he did not have the respect for me that I deserved as his wife. The man who I had devoted my life to did not love me in the way that he should have. It was then that I knew there really was no way back.

★ ★ ★

Our sexuality has been created and given to us by God. The emotions He fills us with help us to express ourselves in communicating with Him and with each other. Our desires to give and receive physical love within a committed relationship are a healthy component within that union and a consequence of God's own desire for us to be fulfilled. We should feel no shame for such feelings. Our physical urges are perfectly natural and the subject should not be considered taboo. For a relationship to succeed both parties need to be content. If at any time one or even both members are unhappy or have concerns, then there is a need for discussion. Being honest about our feelings is an absolutely essential communication within a relationship, however difficult it might seem to instigate.

★ ★ ★

The birds and the bees together with other familiar creatures play a vital role in bringing our garden to its fullness. The foliage alone does not make the garden complete any more than friendship on its own can compensate for the gentle physical love within a mutual and harmonious relationship. The unassuming bumble bee pollinates from flower to flower before taking his nectar to his own hive. Nature has charged him with a responsibility not just for using the pollen to turn into honey, but also to carry vital nutrients from flower to flower which he dispenses as he nuzzles his way in and out of them. The cheerful chirping of young birds as the sun comes up early on a summer morning help to create a pleasurable place of completeness as I anticipate the new day. To hear them singing happily tells me that all is well in my garden and that they (and I) now live in a place of contentment.

WASTE NOT, WANT NOT

Some time later the brook dried up because there had been no rain in the land.

1 Kings 17:7 NIV

During dry seasons when the sun is hot and hosepipes are banned, those of us who have had the forethought to conserve rainwater in outside containers might well be thankful that we have. When the garden becomes lifeless and dry as a result of a shortage of rain such storage can provide instant refreshment. Life may often bring a similar shortfall of resources within our finances, and anything that we are able to put aside for such times can help to ease the burden of those dry spells.

I find it greatly reassuring to have discovered that the Bible reiterates much of what my dad taught me when I was small. Matthew 25 covers the subject of the future and how we should be prepared for whatever lies ahead. In specific details he talks about how there will often be no warning of what is to come and that we should not be misled. Then in Jesus' teaching through the remainder of that chapter, He uses parables which again drive home these points.

As a little girl, one of the valuable lessons I learned from my dad was not to live beyond my means. Under no circumstances would he have allowed me to buy anything before I had enough money to pay for it. "You never know what's around the corner," he would say, "and you might not always be able to keep up repayments if you borrow money in advance." In those days credit cards were not the everyday essential that they have since become, and the 'buy now pay later' age that has been born from them had yet to surface. So for me, the only form of payment available was either cash or my cheque book. These days, it seems normal to pay for our purchases with a credit card and the temptation to take advantage of only meeting the minimum payment at the end of each month can seem an attractive idea. Unfortunately, those who make such a decision are often unaware of the costly interest which is being added to the outstanding balance. *

* * *

When Anthony proposed to me, he was already paying off a bank loan as well as a credit card debt, which was something very new to me. By his own admission he was not good at managing money and for that reason, from the beginning of our marriage, I encouraged him to allow me to take care of the day to day finances. We were married with the debt, but with my money handling experience, we managed to pay it off within the first year. However, almost immediately after we had made the last payment, he took out another loan against my wishes and bought a new stereo system. This was a purchase which I believed was unnecessary, but, in contrast, one which he believed was essential. Up until then I had never been driven by material items, and given my upbringing and the way I had been taught to look after money, I was always ready to wait until I was able to fully fund my purchases. Then, often by the time I had managed to save the money I needed, I no longer wanted the purchase anyway. Once I was married, my priorities became focused on our first child and her needs, and though I did not recognise it initially, it should have been clear from the beginning that Anthony's were different. He enjoyed owning material items and at the time, the good relationship he had with his bank allowed him to fund much of what he wanted in an instant.

---

* An interesting and considerably worrying statistic is, that if a 19-year old spends £3,000 on a credit card at 16% interest and makes only the standard, minimum repayments each month, they will be 46-years old by the time that debt is paid back!

Initially in our day to day life, I did a good job of working out what money was coming in and how much needed to be paid out again and I usually managed to cover the monthly bills with a little bit extra set aside. During the first four or five years of our marriage, I happily took responsibility of making sure we kept our heads above water by shrewdly putting money aside each month to help us adjust to the cost of our planned future mortgage repayments. In less than two years and with much excitement, we were able to buy our first home.

Anthony was really a wheeler-dealer, and always looking for an opportunity to make money. To his credit, in those early years he would sell cars or carry out mechanical repairs to make extra money to bring into the home. He bought our daughter's first pushchair with the money he made by selling a car, and I can remember that he worked late for several nights one December to buy me a watch for Christmas. Those are fond memories as I consider how united we were in those days working together to build a better home for ourselves and our children.

Gradually, Anthony began to move in different circles though, particularly once he had left the British Forces. Though initially he was employed with a regular income, he eventually chose to work for himself and the incoming money became erratic and irregular with many cash transactions that I was often unaware of. I gradually lost control of managing the finances since I was no longer able to keep a track in the same way, and eventually I struggled to make the regular monthly bank payments without a confrontation with him first. When it came to problems with cash flow, Anthony approached them in the same way as he did most other issues. He became aggressive at being questioned and tried to dismiss them rather than address them. I am ashamed to say that this approach also rubbed off on me and in the end I too adopted the same response over our flagging finances. Over a period of time we sank so far into debt that I had no idea how to refloat us. Red letters arrived regularly which were often followed with aggressive phone calls. I knew there were insufficient funds to pay the rising debts, and in the end I stopped opening the mail for fear of what I would read. Dismissing these relentless reminders felt easier to deal with than facing them head on as well as risking another conflict at home. To a great extent it was pointless to ask Anthony for money. If he didn't have it then and there, his way to react to the pressure of being asked was to erupt into a violent fury and turn the situation around so that I felt guilty for asking.

Eventually our gas and electricity supply was cut off because we had not paid the bills, and we were given the option to use a key meter instead. Meters are notoriously expensive to run, but at least it meant we only needed to pay for our utilities as and when we used them, which made things more affordable day by day. However, even then there were times when the credit would run out and we had no available funds to feed into the meter. Then we would spend the evening in the dark with as many candles as we could find.

One thing I could never have comprehended during those years, once I had lost control over our domestic finances, was the vast amount of cash which I later discovered had regularly come into our home without my knowledge. In the spring of 1997, having been employed by a friend during the previous year, Anthony was paid a minimum taxable salary of £8,000. I was aware that this amount was supplemented by a regular amount of cash that had not gone through the books. It was a tax fiddle and once again I turned a blind eye to it. My interests were about keeping the bank manager happy and feeding us all. At that time I had little concern about the repercussions had this ever come to light. Between a week and every ten days, Anthony would supplement what had been paid into the bank with enough cash to keep us going for a while, or until I needed to nag him again. Thankful each time I was paid out, I could never have imagined the amount of money that he had really made. I saw as much as I needed to pay bills with sometimes something extra, and I was content with that (or relieved). However, at the end of that financial year, I discovered that our total income for that year had been more than £35,000! That meant that he had brought as much as £27,000 in cash into our home. It was an astonishing and alarming discovery, because aside from continuing to struggle paying our domestic bills, we had nothing significant to show for such a large amount of income. We had not had a holiday that year or made any considerable purchases for the home or for ourselves. All we appeared to have managed to do was survive. It was impossible for me to contemplate where the money had gone. But it had. Was this all down to poor management? And if so was this my fault for not keeping it under control? Ridiculous though it was, rather than question him and demand to know how we had managed to get through such a large amount of cash with nothing to account for it, I ignored the risk of a fight and instead I took to prayer. In a shameful and shallow way, I began to speak to a God I didn't know and asked that he might make Anthony even more successful the following year and earn £45,000 – £10,000 more coming into our home would surely be enough to make a difference! I really believed that money would solve everything that was wrong in our life.

Each new venture was the one that Anthony believed would make us rich, and being rich was something we both wanted in those days. For me, money would give me security and I believed that security would erase the other issues within our relationship. For Anthony, being rich would give him power and control, and maybe even he believed that it would erase other issues in our life too. My dad often jokingly referred to him as 'Del Boy', and would tease me by quoting "This time next year you'll be millionaires!" Anthony's enthusiasm with each new scheme usually convinced me, for a while at least, that this would be "the one," and whenever I did have reservations, he would reassuringly tell me to trust him. So I did. At one time he became involved in purchasing hundreds of pounds worth of counterfeit items to sell on again with a potentially large profit, but mostly these items went unsold. His contacts seemed to get bored with the same old stuff, or perhaps their conscience would not allow them to buy items that were being exposed on the news as illegal. Police were often swooping in on these sellers' homes, and we were aware that one of Anthony's contacts had been detained in Thailand as he tried to export thousands of pounds worth of counterfeit sportswear back to the UK. With such a surplus stock, our entire wardrobe was at one point made up of fake designer wear that had originally been intended for resale, but instead amounted to surplus supplies and a further damage to our resources.

By the time we had been married for fifteen years, we were in dire straits. We were out of our depth not just with the bank but with credit cards as well as many of the utility suppliers. Anthony had taken on numerous money making schemes over the years, though virtually all had failed to reach fruition. In the past, and in an effort to ease the pressure, we had moved house a few times, either to free up our equity or to take on a new mortgage and reduce the monthly payments. But I was reluctant to move home again because I was afraid that we might end up with no equity or else have a mortgage tied to us in our old age. We fought timelessly over this, but I was determined that we should stay in our home this time. There were not many times when I was brave enough or strong enough to stand my ground, but the arguments over selling up our home were ones where I would not back down. By this time, we lived in a modest three bedroom house with a garden and a garage. It was on a residential estate where the children had many friends, and I was not willing to downgrade and buy a two-up two-down terraced house on a busy main road where the children would not be safe to play outside.

Cars were actually his real passion. He had trained as a mechanic while he was in the Air Force and his hunger to make a profit gave him a tremendous sales pitch. He could buy an old banger, spend a few hours under the bonnet or painting it up, and then sell it on at an enormous profit. I took offence when he made large profits from my family, though his reckoning to this was the same as if it was for any other buyer. "If they think they've had a good deal, then they HAVE had a good deal," he would tell me, and I accepted that I didn't know enough about business to understand how things worked anyway.

When Anthony purchased a nearly new Mercedes from where he worked, he believed he could make a potentially large profit from it. He had paid considerably less than its trade value and expected that he would virtually double his money. However, within a few weeks he discovered that the car had previously been an insurance write-off and its street value was not what he had first believed. In fact it probably wasn't even worth the money he had paid for it. The car looked beautiful and drove very well, but due to the insurance implications, it was not a viable purchase for a prospective buyer. For this reason I suggested that we kept it for ourselves and enjoy the luxury of driving a prestigious car that had cost us very little. For a while that was what we did. I registered and insured the car in my name, and for several months I became known locally as "the lady with the white Mercedes". However, Anthony couldn't settle and, still with his sights set on the large profit, several months later plotted a scheme that left me rigid with fear.

Along with two other friends he arranged to have the car stolen and destroyed, after which he would make a claim against my insurance. I begged him many times to drop this idea both on moral grounds and for the legal implications. It frightened me so much that his plan would go wrong and he could end up in prison. I knew if I was ever questioned by the police I would not be able to lie, and it was unfair that he should put me under that pressure. It is almost impossible for me to express exactly how frightened I was at that time as I considered the possible consequences if his plan were to backfire. Because of the implications of confiding with anyone else, I felt under more pressure than I had ever known as I struggled alone with the fear of what could happen, as well as my conscience and knowing in my heart that what he was contemplating was very wrong.

I pleaded with him to change his mind and to consider the implications on us and in particular our two children. If he went to prison, they would not only suffer the endurance of losing their daddy for a while, but would also be humiliated or bullied at school once the other children found out what had happened. None of my pleas dissuaded him, and finally one evening he took the car to a friend's house and the deed was done. Fortunately the police felt there was no need to contact me as they were convinced by whatever Anthony told them. The insurance paid out over £15,000, which he used mostly to buy more cars to sell on at a profit. In hindsight, I am certain that this incident allowed the cracks within our marriage to widen further. The fear of his plan going wrong had consumed me for many months, and my emotions had been torn between trying to convince myself that Anthony's theory that what he had done was not such a big deal, and fighting with my conscience and all the moral lessons I had learned as a child. Deep in my heart, I knew that it was very wrong indeed, but I was too afraid and too ashamed to share this with anyone or even admit my own feelings to myself. One of my greatest concerns was that he could have found himself in deeper water than he was able to swim in. In whatever way I view him now, at that time when we were married, I also knew a softer person within him. He was the man I loved and the idea of my husband having to live among real criminals who were really bad people frightened me beyond explanation. It had never crossed my mind that my awareness of his plan could have also implicated me and that there was a chance that I too could have ended up in prison.

★ ★ ★

After my uncle died, I inherited a large sum of money. Since holidays had always been scarce or were booked on a tight budget, I imagined us using some of the money to take the children to Disneyland in Paris, or even further afield to America. None of us had ever done anything like that, and I considered how beneficial it would be for us to spend time together away from all the usual pressures. However, on the very same day that my mum and dad dropped the cheque round, Anthony clearly had his own ideas and made an appointment to view a Rolls Royce. Out of nowhere, I was advised of a business venture to chauffeur wedding parties which he had apparently always wanted to have a go at, and our windfall would give him the opportunity to set it up. Once again, I was given in long detail all the amazing reasons why this venture was fail-proof. Though I was completely against it from the start because it would take up half of the money immediately, Anthony continued to promote his business plan to me. I suggested my idea of a holiday, which would give us some time to think about what we should do with our investment, and also suggested we use some of the capital to pay off a chunk of the mortgage to bring the monthly outgoings down. Anthony's mind was made up however, and all he had to do was to convince me that the new business was a feasible and profitable idea. And once again he did. Or at least I gave in.

On the very day that the cheque cleared, Anthony made his new purchase which used up more than half of the money. The wedding hire business was never destined to work, just like so many other ventures that Anthony took on. The cost of running the Rolls Royce, complete with a chauffeur, meant the profits were minimal, and the competition from other established businesses was too great. The car spent much of its time parked on our front driveway and was occasionally used for us to take novelty trips to the theatre. Several years later I was somewhat devastated when I learned that on one occasion my dad had asked him if he could use the car as a treat to take my mum to the theatre in it for their anniversary. Anthony agreed and organised a driver, and charged my dad £200!

Eventually, after a couple of years, I actually managed to persuade him to cut his losses and sell the car. We lost more than £4,000 on the original purchase price plus the costs it had incurred while we had owned it. I thought at least that this would put some money back into our pot, but instead of taking money for the sale, he arranged a deal with a couple of car traders to do a swap with three or four cars to sell on. I never saw any of the original investment returned, and so it was that another large chunk of money never made it to our water butt.

The remainder of my uncle's legacy originally went into a

separate savings account so that it did not get swallowed up into our unstable domestic finances. After a while, Anthony realised that this made it difficult to access the money because we had no cheque book for that account. Therefore, it seemed sensible to open a second current account which would still be separate from our other affairs. After he visited the bank to set up this account, I was shocked when he returned and advised me that he had not been able to open an account in joint names because I had accrued some adverse credit. This was the first I had ever heard of this, but at the time I was running a small printing business, which wasn't greatly successful. Though my bills were normally paid on time and I had no previous understanding that I had built up such a reputation, I was also aware that cash flow was a bit tight and I assumed this was how such an adversity had managed to build up. In any case, it didn't seem such a big deal, because Anthony's credit rating was apparently okay, so there would be no problem opening up an account in his name only. To me that made perfect sense. A few weeks later, having made the decision to buy a second house to rent out, once again my 'adverse credit' caused a problem when we applied for a joint mortgage. Again it seemed sensible to overcome this hurdle by agreeing that Anthony should take on the mortgage in his name.

Three years later, after I had left him and during a time when I had neither any money, nor a job, I went to the bank to make a small withdrawal from the joint savings account and discovered there was a balance of just ninety-four pence! In disbelief at what the bank were telling me, I requested a complete set of bank statements from when the account had originally been opened, which confirmed that over those three years Anthony had gradually withdrawn all of the money and transferred it either into the account he had set up in his own name or else he had made cash withdrawals. I had not made one transaction. I was immediately advised to put a land order on the second home. Because my name did not appear on the deeds due to my 'adverse credit', there was a chance that Anthony could sell it without my knowledge and if he did, there was little I would be able to do about it. As his wife I was legally entitled to fifty per cent of any equity, but as only his name was linked to the mortgage, and in view of my shattering discovery, I could no longer trust anything he might do. My dry season had arrived, and I had nothing stored in my water butt.

These are extreme examples of badly managed finances and they also highlight my own weakness in not being willing to recognise my first husband's dishonesty and capability to control at any cost. People find themselves in debt for many reasons and there are times when it is genuinely out of their control. Long term sickness can result in a greatly reduced income, redundancy or even retirement all mean that budgets need to be adjusted and lifestyle changes made. However, if we cut our cloth accordingly and try to live within our means, it is possible to keep ourselves afloat and even have a small water butt to store for a dry spell in most circumstances.

★ ★ ★

Despite the love I have developed in my relationship with God, I still question why some people have so much while others appear to struggle. This is a question that concerns both Christians and non-Christians alike. To the non-Christian it can be one of the very reasons that will interfere with them taking their leap of faith. But I have come to accept that God does not need us to have the answers to all of His plans. The essence of faith is trust. It is true that some people appear to be blessed in great abundance while others are handed a more humble lifestyle. I do believe that God always has a reason for this, even if we are unable to understand it for ourselves. It is also fair to say that God is not responsible for the choices we make, and we need to be accountable for our own decisions. God promises us through faith that He will not leave us, He doesn't promise to protect us from our wrong choices. How we deal with them is all part of developing our faith.

Whatever troubles me these days, I try to work at through prayer.

Even so, God doesn't always (or even usually) respond immediately, and there have been times when I have wondered whether He actually hears me at all. Eventually, I come to realise that He never lets me down. Rather, He sits on the sidelines for a while and waits for me to do some thinking for myself. He wants me to be accountable, just like any other parent would ask of their child.

As I write this, I feel drawn to the story of Joseph and how God warned him through a series of dreams that a famine would follow years of plenty. There were some that prepared for that famine and some that didn't. However, God had given warning through Joseph so that all preparations could be made. It is important to understand that God did not send the famine first. Instead, He made sure there were first seven years of plenty, which was more than enough time to harvest and adjust for the predicted shortage. Of course, it is not possible to build up resources all of the time. Inevitably there will always be dry periods in our lives when we have to live from day to day and are unable to think beyond tomorrow. But when the climate changes and the crops begin to yield, it is useful if we are mindful of our water butt and prepare for another unexpected dry season.

By living within my means and trying to be prepared for any eventuality, I am now blessed with a modest reserve, which is adequate to my needs. If Anthony and I had managed our money carefully during those years of plenty, our resources and stability would have been much greater. Anthony was not a good husband, and though he appeared to love his children, he often neglected their needs for the sake of his own self-indulgence and a desire to be able to do things that were important to him. This selfishness was a form of greed, though not as obvious as the greed he portrayed when he neglected to keep our home financially stable.

As a Christian, one of the important lessons I have learned is that money will not make me happy. There is a line between aiming to have enough to cover our necessary needs and that of lusting over the meaningless material items that we sometimes yearn for. We live in a fast and aggressive world where emphasis is often placed on material values over moral ones. I love these words of Dale Carnegie, which remind me to slow down and enjoy the season while it's here: "So many of us are dreaming of some magical rose garden over the horizon – instead of enjoying the roses that are blooming outside our window today!"

Equally useful for me are the words of The Apostle Paul who wrote in: 1 Timothy: 6 'The love of money is the root of all kinds of evil'. So often this phrase has been misquoted to suggest that 'money is the root of all evil'. But I have come to understand that money is not the problem, only the love of it.

When I first turned to God in prayer, I was desperate, lonely and in debt. Never having taken the time to understand who He really is, I expected Him to love me enough to reward me with as much money as would clear my debts and give me a fresh start. It was incredibly shallow and I am ashamed, even as I write this, that I was unable to recognise how money orientated I had become. I really did believe that a large enough windfall would solve my problems and restore my happiness. The reality was that lack of money was only a small part of the big picture. There were many other issues which needed addressing before I had even the smallest chance of finding contentment. As I gradually reached an intimacy with God, I discovered that money would not take away those issues and actually such a windfall would only act as a further burden just as it clearly had when I received my inheritance. The money which was left to me by my uncle had given Anthony buying power to purchase even more unnecessary material items and, instead of taking the time to fully consider how to use it wisely, his greed had left us in greater financial turmoil.

The Bible asks us to love God above all others and forsake all other gods. As I prayed that He would replenish our bank account, it never occurred to me at that time that money had become my 'god'.

The water butt in my garden is situated at the side of the house. In winter it fills to overflowing, then during the summer it serves as a thirst quenching tonic for the shrubs and flowers when the sun is hot and the rain is scarce. It is only due to forward planning that I am blessed with this regular supply to rely on when the ground is dry. Without it, the generous gift of an April shower would trickle away and be wasted.

★ ★ ★

Not long before this book went to publication I became involved in a wonderful organisation called Christians Against Poverty (CAP). It was a series of events that stirred my passion towards this cause, and led me to become a very proud CAP Money Coach, helping people to re-discover the basic money management principles that can make the difference between sinking or staying afloat. The CAP Money courses that we have so far run in our own community have proved hugely helpful to the delegates, and have enabled them to organise their finances which ultimately give them a greater chance of keeping out of debt. I would encourage anyone who feels that their finances could be improved to think about taking advantage of attending a CAP Money course. Through the generosity of these fully trained, volunteer money coaches, we have seen course centres opening up and down the country. Each team of coaches are warm, unobtrusive and completely confidential. The courses run for three consecutive weeks and are all run free of charge.

In addition to the CAP Money courses, which are designed to help manage finances, another aspect of the work of CAP is that of the CAP Debt Centres. These centres are again run by fully trained debt coaches who work alongside fully trained debt councillors at CAP's head office in Bradford. Debt coaches visit people in their own homes offering a much needed face to face service to people who are experiencing real debt issues. Often these people are being chased for money that they are unable pay back, which can have devastating consequences on self esteem and relationships. CAP are now recognised among most of the money lenders in the credit industry and because of this, they are often able to negotiate better terms and ultimately take all the pressure away from the client. CAP's debt counselling service is especially unique because they give each person a special CAP Account to manage all their debt repayments and even bills if necessary. They stay with their clients until they are totally debt free, and give support through the insolvency processes if required. Debt can have devastating effects, sometimes driving people to consider suicide. Through CAP's help many people's lives have been transformed, even saved. For more information visit: www.capuk.org

LOVE YOUR LAWN

Let my teaching fall like rain and my words descend like dew, like showers on new grass, like abundant rain on tender plants.

Deuteronomy 32:2 NIV

People who suffer with self confidence issues can have a tendency to overvalue what they are not and undervalue what they really are. By that, I mean that they might focus on the things which they don't like about themselves instead of looking at those things which are positive features, and other people love about them. Like many women, through much of my adult life my weight has been an issue to me. Women and their weight! So many of us are unjustly critical of our bodies, and are greatly influenced by airbrushed pictures on magazine covers or the images which can be seen on TV. Often if there is underlying unhappiness in other areas of our lives, the added mental pressure at never being able to compete with such images can cause our self esteem to plummet further as we consider ourselves to be failing, fat and worthless.

Women in general are often under great pressure as they focus on their role within the family. In a household where the husband is the financial provider, his input is essential in keeping the home economically stable. The responsibility of catering for the everyday needs of young children and the day to day running of a home often falls on the woman, and there can be a greater pressure on her if, in addition, she also holds down a job outside the home. With inbuilt nurturing skills and so many responsibilities, her own personal needs can very often be overlooked as she strives to be successful in her role as a housewife and mother. Even in a happy, loving relationship there is still a danger of her losing some of her identity if she is unable to find enough time to spend on herself. Her role can easily be taken for granted and all too quickly, and without realising, she might experience a drain on her confidence or even feel a loss of identity.

Much like the housewife, the lawn is often the focal point of the garden. As the centrepiece, it can often make up the largest area and will be subjected to all kinds of abuse. We can cut it and trim it to keep it tidy, but throughout its life it is often shown little respect as children use it to build dens and play games on, and even by our pets who use it only for their convenience! Without the attention and love that it deserves, all too quickly bald or dry patches will appear and ugly weeds can sprout up. In order to restore it to its rich, green colour it will require a generous helping of TLC. Fortunately, repair can be quickly affected, but a lawn that has been abused long-term will need greater attention to restore it.

★ ★ ★

When my own self worth was at a particularly low point, had I been asked if I knew what made me most unhappy, I would probably have said my weight. Any other issues would have appeared less significant at that time as I battled mentally with myself to try to justify the excess pounds. At one point, I would have been considered as obese, but I was in complete denial and believed I was not necessarily that big. I was however, unhealthily large. Obese is when a person's weight puts their health at risk, and though I was not aware of it, my health was very much at risk. My life style at that time was out of control with late night eating and many fast-food meals each week. Such uncontrolled living was silently putting pressure on me internally as well as externally. It may be that my eating habits were a comfort, though I didn't necessarily think that at the time. My first husband was a picky eater and because he stayed up well into the small hours, he would often eat a late night takeaway while he sat in front of the TV, and I too got into these unhealthy eating habits, often eating fast food just before I went to bed. On the occasions when we went out in the evening, we would seldom come home without a kebab or burgers and chips, which again I would eat with him shortly before I went to bed. It was absolute gluttony, which I am fully ashamed of now when I consider what I was doing to myself. But the food was often a comfort in a life where I often felt greatly neglected, and at other times I would consider it a reward for having kept healthier earlier in the day or during the week.

An already high-fat diet with the regular addition of late night kebabs began to cause a strain on my heart which I was oblivious to at the time, and in addition I was putting myself at risk of other conditions such as high blood pressure or even diabetes. The long term effects from that type of living can interfere with day to day life and my vitality became lost and my lethargy even more pronounced. With the addition of a deepening depression and low self-esteem, it had created a rather concerning cocktail with lethal implications. The damage I was doing to myself was not just physical, I became mentally weary as a result of the increasing pressures in my marriage and the deepening depression I was sinking into. Collectively they set a vicious circle of self-loathing alongside a desperate need to be loved.

I tried so many diets, but in the midst of such a mental mess I found it impossible to stick to any one plan. Not understanding the health risks at that time, and in a relationship where I never felt as though I was worthy of the love I craved, I had no real incentive to stick at it. At one time I concluded that jogging was the way forward. I devised a plan where I would run to one lamp post and walk to the next, alternating them equally, covering a 400 metre circuit. Gradually, I intended to increase the running part to two lamp posts and so on as I became fitter. My first and only attempt was hard going, but I managed to complete the circuit as planned. However, by the time I got back to the house, I was in real trouble. For several minutes I had to fight for my breath. I was actually hyperventilating. It was a hideous and frightening sight as I gasped for breath trying to fill my lungs with air and growling like a sea lion in my panic. It was a petrifying situation and brought me to the verge of a panic attack. My face was scarlet and my eyes bulged in fear, but even after I regained my composure the shock of discovering how unhealthy and unfit I had become was not enough to determine me into doing something positive to change my unhealthy lifestyle. Instead, I blamed my approaching middle age (I was thirty-six), accepted that running was not for me and allowed the experience to drain my confidence further.

It wasn't long before it failed completely. Then, the lower I sank, the more I ate. The bigger I became, the worse I felt, and so on. I have since heard of so many women caught up in that same depressing trap. Never at that time did it occur to me that my weight was only a consequence of the real issues that I had yet to acknowledge. My lifestyle was sapping away my mental strength. The gentle, subtle control that my first husband had mastered perfectly had dragged me to a point of complete neediness. I felt totally worthless and my only comfort was the food I gorged and the compensation of believing that, despite my ugliness, at least my husband stood by me. Through my misery, and with rose coloured glasses, I was fully dependent on what I considered to be my happy marriage. I was completely loyal because my relationship meant everything to me, it was all I had. I continued to believe that we were happy together and because Anthony's taunts were so subtle I was unable to recognise their serious implications on my state of mind. This, I later learned, is exactly what a controller desires.

As a young child, I had been wafer-thin with spindly legs and knobbly knees! In fact, I had been positively underweight until adolescence when I began to fill out. After my children were born in my early twenties, I gained several more pounds, as many women do. My husband made regular comments to this, which rather than being encouraging were insensitive and damaging. I longed to feel attractive to him, but without his support and reassurance I contented myself instead with gorging my way through an increasing depression.

For more than ten years I was unable to break the circuit, convinced that at almost forty I had approached a time in my life when it was inevitable that I would look that way. I hated what I saw in the mirror, so I tried not to look at my reflection. I avoided letting my husband see me undressed because I was ashamed of what I had become. Instead I focused on my gorgeous daughter. In her beautiful adolescence she was beginning to develop into a perfectly shaped young woman. She reminded me of how I had been at her age, and with no interest in buying stylish clothes for my own out of shape body, I took pride instead in helping her to choose outfits and makeup to enhance her beauty. I was so proud of her, and there were times when I believed that people would be amazed at my daughter's natural beauty, considering what an unattractive mother I was. She was my success, and along with her brother they were the two things that I knew I had been good at! For everything that I had failed in, I had at least produced two beautiful children.

Such a pattern of thought is typical of a person who lacks self-confidence. Where they feel undeserving of themselves, they will take comfort in pouring their energies into something or someone whom they believe to be more valuable than they are. It is a denial of realistically accepting the problem in order to block out the pain that comes with it.

Believing that I was ugly on the outside, I made myself ugly on the inside too. I didn't believe that anyone would like me for who I was, and I imagined that they tolerated me only because of their friendships with Anthony and my children. I travelled along a road of self-destruction, not knowing how to divert and much of the time not wanting to. I gave people every reason not to like me, but then crumbled at the thought of being so unpopular. I spent a great deal of time worrying about what other people thought of me, when what I really should have been doing was learning to love and understand myself. It is impossible to love yourself when there seems nothing worth loving, and in my naïve mind I considered it greatly conceited that anyone should claim that they could love themselves. With this thought pattern, I continued to journey along the 'self-destruction road' and consumed all kinds of junk food and negative thoughts on my way.

How then did I manage to divert and find another route? By discovering that I had an underlying, hidden asset, which was my strength of character. Something which had become completely suppressed over the years and I was hardly aware of. Though I was still not acquainted with Him, I know now that God had been with me throughout my whole journey. Despite at times being in what felt like the most difficult of places, I had never been alone. All that had happened to me over the years had been a planned lesson that He had provided for my healthy future.

Shortly after I turned forty, I remember consciously considering that, God willing, I might live another forty years. It occurred to me that, at that time, I was still only halfway through my life. With as many years in front of me as I had already lived, I finally realised I needed more from life. At that point I had no idea what that might be, but I did know I needed something different than I had at that time. In the coming months, even though God had still not openly revealed Himself to me, I began to develop a new healthier mindset and, without any conscious effort, the first positive result of that was a drop in weight by several pounds. Suddenly, I found myself on a different journey, this one was encouraging and I could see something good at the end. I suddenly felt there was hope, and I began to slowly recognise small, but positive things about myself. My focus on prayer changed, and I began to develop a new intimacy with God. I started to talk to Him more openly, and instead of bargaining and begging for material things, I found things to be thankful for. Being thankful, sometimes for just the smallest things, uplifted me and I was aware that there were periods when I felt genuinely cheerful. As my relationship with God developed, I realised that through sincere prayer, He listened and strengthened me, and I felt encouraged to consider that the future could be brighter.

Finally He called me, and, once He had my attention, He used the most prominent people in my life as a channel to strengthen me further. My parents, who I had spent much time avoiding for fear of their disappointment and criticism, showed me more support than I deserved, but their relentless encouragement was everything I needed to begin to turn my life around. They became part of the backbone in building the new me.

The early days of my repair brought about even more turmoil for a while. The weeds and the worms can attack from every vulnerable angle, and my new confidence took one battering after another as I contemplated making decisions about my future. However, within just a few months I finally mustered up the courage and strength I needed to make the decision that would ultimately change my life forever. I moved out of my loveless marriage in an effort to restore my independence again. That moment of leaving everything I had known for twenty years without any real ideas as to where my future would take me, as well as knowing that my children were too old for me to expect them to come with me, was without doubt the most difficult thing I have ever faced. Ten years on, even though I have a completely different life of security and love, I still struggle with periods where I feel intensely guilty at how they may have been affected by what I did for my own sanity. Though it was an almost unbearable wrench, it was without question the right thing to do both for myself and for Anthony. Whether he would ever be honest enough to admit it I don't know, but being married to me had become too restricting for him. He needed the freedom to do his own things without the worry of a nagging and miserable wife questioning him constantly. We had reached a point in our lives where we wanted different things and our morals and standards were no longer compatible.

★ ★ ★

When we are hurting, there is often the temptation to find a 'quick fix' which will take away the pain. Regrettably, deep rooted issues will not properly heal with a quick remedy. Instead, it will only paper over the cracks, which in time will tear open again leaving us exposed once more. The saying 'it will get worse before it gets better' was never more true for me than when I first left Anthony. The lead up to my divorce was frightening and intimidating as he continued to play regular mind games with me, and the divorce itself was painfully long-winded due to Anthony's reluctance to accept defeat. Without God pouring regular doses of inner strength into me, and the assurance that many of the people I loved most were standing beside me, I would never have worked through the intensity of those times and my sanity would have come into question yet again. The road to 'recovery' was even more enduring than the road to 'self destruction' had ever been, because on that road at least I was unaware of what was actually happening. On my recovery journey, I had become conscious of what was going on around me, either in a new way, or often for the first time, and it was often unbearably painful.

As I reflect on that time of both survival and healing, I am now mindful of how it helped me to discover so much about myself. Just as importantly, I have learned how much God loves me. He loves every one of us, including those who have yet to recognise Him. When people tell me that they don't believe in God, I reassure them that thankfully, "God believes in them." He doesn't love us on merit, and none of us are any more or less worthy to Him. He loves us the way we are, because the way we are is how He made us! Once I accepted that God loved the inferior, unworthy me, I was finally able to understand how to love myself. I found reassurance in recognising one or two encouraging features in me at first, and held on to them. As with an exhausted lawn, no matter how unloved and battered it has been, just a small amount of care will give encouraging results and in acknowledging a few positive features in myself, my confidence began to be restored. Slowly.

When I thought about my ugly body, I remembered that in my younger years I had often been complimented for my shapely legs. Over the years they had become heavier with the rest of me, but they still had good shape. These small but encouraging thoughts ignited enough spark for me to be more rational in my thinking. The initial few pounds that I had lost were enough incentive for me to actively work at losing some more. It was no longer as difficult because I felt incentivised, and I soon believed that my shapely legs could look good again! Every positive thought that I was able to pour into myself helped me to take another constructive step forward. Albeit small ones, but in the right direction.

★ ★ ★

With the previous road now far behind me, I can acknowledge with some shame the dreadful person I had allowed myself to be during that time. I am naturally a sensitive soul and because of that I am also perceptive to the needs of others. This quality had helped to make me a good mother. During the years of the ugly person I had created, I was too consumed in my own issues to be considerate to those of others. I have a sharp wit, but again, through my lost years, that sense of humour had also left me. Anthony took delight in laughing at other people's expense and, ashamedly, I admit that I often joined in with him. I am not proud of these failings, but in order to overcome all my demons I have needed to be completely honest with myself.

Before I made the courageous decision to leave my marriage, I could not have worked harder at trying to save it. My attempts were endless but in the end they were not enough. Our marriage was in deeper trouble than Anthony was willing to admit, so he could not appreciate what needed to be done to put it back together. Booking the appointment with the counsellor proved more eye opening than I could have expected at the time. I went there only in response to Anthony's angry outburst after I questioned his relationship with our friend. I am certain that he had not considered the impact the appointment would have on both of us. It was a rare occasion for Anthony to come off second, but that was one which backfired.

A woman of a similar age to me greeted me at the door and escorted me to a quiet room. I had gone there believing that the problems within my relationship were my fault and had mentally prepared myself for being told some home truths. Even so, I had to be honest with her, because there was so much at stake. At that time, I didn't want my husband to leave me and to have to come to terms with being abandoned again. It was a great comfort to discover that a counsellor doesn't work by giving home truths. Instead, she listened patiently as I poured out eighteen years of confusion and frustration. The tears flowed heavily throughout the session, and I lost all composure on realising only through hearing my own words, that I was not totally responsible for the rift in my marriage.

She said very little, the clarity came from me. She only suggested that from what I had told her, Anthony seemed a little self-centred with some manipulating traits. I actually didn't know at that point what manipulating meant and I had to look it up. 'Controlling, influential and dominant', these are all words that fairly describe my first husband well. The entry in Dictionary.com reads the word manipulating as: 'to influence or manage shrewdly or deviously'. That again describes him accurately. Imagine that for all those years as his wife I had not recognised that he had been controlling me!

Her main advice was that I should consider spending some time for myself to create a better sense of well being. She could see so much of what I had been blind to. For far too long my focus had been on the needs of Anthony and my children. My own needs had long been put on the back burner as I had carried out my role as a wife and mother.

"It seems to me that you have allowed yourself to be completely put upon. Everyone is demanding from you, and you have little time to consider what you want for yourself," she told me. "I suggest you consider making some time once or twice a week just for you. During that 'you' time, do not allow anyone to disturb or interrupt whatever you have decided to do. You don't have to do anything extravagant. You don't even need to be away from the home. You would be surprised what a difference it will make if you invest in a luxury bubble bath and some scented candles. Then lock yourself away in your bathroom and don't allow anyone to ask anything of you while you relax and indulge in your bath."

I was unable to remember the last time I had been selfish enough to put my own needs first, but that evening I took her advice and the effects were immediate. Thirty uninterrupted minutes of indulgence with only my own thoughts, and without demands from my family, was a new experience and I immersed in it. Luxury baths became a regular feature in my week from then on, and with the door locked, I could think clearly in my own company. It was during those times of peace that I began to really talk to God. Anthony shone in a new light and I recognised some of his failings within our relationship. At that time I still could not consider a life without him, but for the first time I accepted the troubles in our marriage were not all down to me. I acknowledged that he did not always treat me fairly or indeed our children. I spent many, many months from then on trying to pull our marriage back on track. I wanted it to work more than anything and, even after his affair with our friend, I was prepared to dismiss it and build on what we still had.

Anthony never asked me what happened at the counselling, and I only felt the need to go there twice. After that I was able to think more clearly for myself, and when I needed to spend time mulling something over, I went off on my own and had a bath. I had hoped that we would have gained greatly by having some sessions as a couple, but when I suggested that, he had no desire for it. I made several attempts to organise time on our own, but almost defiantly he made other arrangements around our friends or with the children.

Finally, it was obvious to me that I had nothing to stay for. My daughter was in a steady relationship with her boyfriend, and I knew that my son wasn't far behind her in becoming a young adult. When I imagined that within a few years they would be leaving home, I found very little that enticed me to stay. I had searched my soul to work at making significant, positive changes within me in order to save our marriage, but Anthony had not, and I concluded that he never would.

It is said, 'What doesn't kill us will make us stronger', and this was never more appropriate than it was for me. I am stronger now than I have ever been and I believe that strength has only manifested itself because of the things I needed to overcome. When I do falter, I have God's wonderful promise to hold on to. However difficult our circumstances, He only sets us trials that we are able to bear. He does this to test us and to gift us with inner strength so that we are able to overcome our problems as well as to help us appreciate everything we have. In times of plenty and when life is good, it is easy for us to become complacent. Through daily prayer, God helps me to be grateful and to overcome my own natural urge to take what I have for granted.

★ ★ ★

Malc and I have very different reasons to be thankful for what we have. He has not experienced unhappiness within a relationship like I have, and his pain is far different to any that I have encountered, but equally our situations have helped us to appreciate that we have been truly blessed with a second chance to be happy. Our past experiences, though different from each others, have made us conscious not to take each other or our relationship for granted. We work hard at making each other happy and being considerate of each other's needs. I have enough confidence in myself to know that I am a very worthy and needed person in his life. There are still days when I find myself at a low point, and that is a consequence of what happened in my first marriage. Without question, because of our pasts, our approach towards each other within our relationship has made us stronger, more considerate people in general. And in retrospect, our past trials have unquestionably had a positive effect on our personalities and the people that we have now become.

The football pitch is probably one of the most prominently abused lawns I can think of. For eight months or more it takes a weekly battering from men wearing studded boots fighting for possession of the ball. During the game little respect is given to its needs as they slide across the surface kicking out lumps of turf. At the end of the season, the consequences are apparent with huge bare patches particularly in the goal mouth where much of the action takes place. The closed season is only a few months through the summer, but within that time the grounds man and his team work hard to restore the pitch to pristine condition for the start of the new season.

My small garden lawn is rich and green in colour. Like the football pitch it wasn't always like that. It looks happy because Malc and I spend time pampering it. It is fed regularly and sufficiently watered when required. We trim it weekly in the growing season and remove all blemishes by uplifting any weeds. This regular makeover is as important to the lawn as it is for me to spend a small, but regular amount of time on myself so that I can hold on to my identity and feel comfortable enough with myself to overcome tough times that, in my former life, would have left me feeling like the end of season football pitch.

THE THORNS ON THE ROSES

No longer will the people of Israel have malicious neighbours who are painful briers and sharp thorns. Then they will know that I am God.
Ezekiel 28v24 NIV

Roses in a garden are a wonderful blessing, and with a range of extensive varieties they bring colour and fragrance with highly perfumed flowers that can last throughout the whole summer. They are reliably hardy and long lasting, returning year after year. As with our friends, we seem to enjoy them more and more as they mature and develop, producing larger bouquets as the years pass. Their one obvious downside are the thorns which run along their stems and can prick sharply without warning. Therefore, you need to handle them with care and respect to avoid being pricked.

Friendships need to be built on trust, and like roses, as the relationship grows and trust is born, they should begin to create something similar to that of the rose: something beautiful and fragrant, but hardy enough to withstand all weathers time and again, and thereby enlightening our lives with their fragrant, reliable companionship. I can think of just a few people whose friendship can be compared to a summer rose in that way, and in recent years I have become so thankful for the blessing of such real friendship. When we are vulnerable and searching affirmation to a situation, those true friends who are willing to stand by and support us with honest advice, can often help us to clarify that which on our own seems unfair or unclear. Listening ears and sound advice, however harsh it might appear to us at first, can help to release the greatest of burdens if we have trust in the one that we choose to share with. At the same time, we may sometimes find that our offloading can become overwhelming to some as they struggle with the pressure of having to keep our confidentiality. Their intentions may have been genuine in the beginning, but perhaps they don't agree with everything we have told them and they find themselves somewhat overwhelmed or feel that they are expected to agree with us when they don't. Sadly, those same friends might even believe they are helping the situation by acting on our behalf, when in reality their act of 'loyalty' only creates further problems. Or perhaps we have simply put our trust in someone too soon, without having discovered either how trustworthy they are or where they fit in to the situation that is troubling you. When it seems as though so much is against us, it's understandable that we will try and round up our allies. In a vulnerable place, we might be much quicker to try to achieve this than is right for us, and we risk putting our confidence into people who we either don't know well enough, or mistrusted.

My sister-in-law had been my close friend since we were teenagers. She understood the problems in my relationship because she had grown up with Anthony and had known his character all her life. She had also witnessed many of the hurtful comments and inappropriate behaviour he had directed towards me many times. In that final year, just a few months before I left him, I had a holiday with her and it was during that time that I shared with her my most intimate dreams and fears. The release was tremendously strengthening as she confirmed things which I already knew in my heart and just needed to hear from someone else; that my stale marriage was not all my fault. Highlighting to me that there was fault on both sides, gave me a fighting spirit to try to help Anthony acknowledge that we had much to do if we were to pull our marriage back. I definitely wanted to do that and was fully armoured to overcome whatever battle lay ahead, though I knew it would need to begin by gently outlining my suggestions that we needed to make significant changes. I believed that by taking this gentle approach I would get his attention and we could begin to rediscover each other without the need for a battle.

This seems unimaginably idyllic as I write it, and I know now that it would never have panned out in that way. Anthony would not have allowed me to convince him that he had failings and that he was not always a good husband. Admitting he was wrong was something he rarely did, and if I had suggested that there was fault on both sides he would have turned everything back onto me in his usual familiar style.

At the same time that I confided in my sister-in-law, I had also begun talking to other people, men and women in a chat room on the Internet. The online conversations were a great escapism as I was able to interact with people who were willing to relate with me. It was easy for me to be open with people in this way, because with a computer screen between us I could say anything I liked without concern that my confessions would ever come back on me because the 'friend' behind the screen would never know me or my family personally. In time though, I took that friendship a step further and occasionally met up with a crowd of the 'roomies' for a pub lunch, which often rolled on into the evening. In hindsight, these friendships were shallow and one sided. All of us had similar issues and were chasing the same dreams and escapism. Most were in unhappy relationships and had lost their self-confidence, just like me. I really felt I had something in common with these people at first, and because of that it was easy to build relationships and believe that they were people I could trust. Some were just desperate to have a fairytale relationship at almost any cost and believed that the chat room was where they would find it. Others (like me) had very little confidence and such interaction helped to create a self-belief that had long been lost. All of us though, were looking for an impossible solution to our unhappiness by mixing with people who we would normally have nothing in common with. Then when a person of the opposite sex paid us the smallest amount of attention, we were romanced into believing that we had met our perfect match.

I was as romanced as anyone. Several times, men made passes at me and even when I was not attracted to them, either by their picture or their conversation, my confidence was raised just because someone had actually paid me some attention. At one of the regular lunches I did meet a man who I immediately warmed to. We spent the whole afternoon talking and flirting with each other. It felt wonderful to be in the company of a man who constantly flattered me. After that first lunch we began to speak together online and eventually swapped mobile phone numbers. We met a couple more times at the lunches and a friendship developed which was certain to lead me into temptation. I knew that, but I was drugged by his charm and interest in me.

In all of my married years I had never contemplated being unfaithful. It had never crossed my mind. I am naturally monogamous and I continued to be convinced that I had everything I needed in my husband (even in the depths of unhappiness). I would never have considered taking such a risk which might result in me losing everything. However, the Internet arrived at a time when I had found myself putting questions against my marriage, and the regular meetings and conversations with other men and women helped to clarify the aspects of it that were making me unhappy. So when this man flirted with me, I was more flattered than I should have been, and soaked up his compliments like a sponge. When he suggested that we meet for an evening on our own, I agreed without thinking the consequences through thoroughly. Even the fear of Anthony finding out did not deter me. I was ignited by the fantasy of a forthcoming night of intimacy with a man who desired me and would release my locked up passions.

Unable to keep my secret completely to myself, I shared it with my sister-in-law, who told me I was on a rocky road, but even so she said that she understood why I felt so drawn. I knew she was right and underneath I did become very afraid of the consequences. If Anthony found out our marriage would be over for sure, and I was also afraid of being in such an intimate situation with a man I did not really know. I had not been seen undressed in many years and was greatly conscious of the extra weight I carried around my middle. Even so, I continued to fantasise in fairytale style at the thought of being caressed and adored. I called my sister-in-law constantly, informing her of every minor detail time and again, just for reassurance.

The morning before my planned date, I was heading into town when I got a call from Anthony on my mobile phone. He seemed agitated and was not happy that I was not at home. He told me he had some important cheques that needed banking and told me to come back straight away. I knew immediately that he was unhappy about something and it crossed my mind that he suspected my plans. I have never been a good liar, so I must have been perfectly transparent to him. When I got home he was waiting for me, and my sixth sense told me that he knew about my plans, and I was absolutely petrified of what would happen if I was right. I had previously lied, and told him I was going to stay with a girlfriend the following night, but when he asked me that morning who the girlfriend was I knew he had rumbled me. I didn't lie anymore, there was no point. An ugly scene erupted as I tried to justify what had driven me to my planned infidelity. In a strange way I was relieved that he had discovered the truth. It crossed my mind that this might be the catalyst he needed to finally appreciate how troubled our marriage was. At that stage I had not yet actually been unfaithful, and I wouldn't have needed to follow it through if the two of us could have finally sat down and talked our problems out. But nothing I said made any difference. Once again, Anthony used his temper to intimidate me and make himself completely blameless in this situation. He conveniently overlooked his own infidelity with our friend just a year before, which he had lied about and denied when I had confronted him. At the end of that terrible row, Anthony told me our marriage was over and made me leave the house. Unknowing when or even whether he would allow me back home again, I had no idea what to do. I cancelled my arrangements for the following evening and spent the day at a friend's house as I tried to reflect on everything Anthony had hurled at me in his anger, and I tried to work out in my head how I would ever manage to repair the damage I had caused by my plans.

By late afternoon, Anthony had called me demanding me to come home and arrange a meal for him and the children. I took this as an opportunity to do some serious grovelling in the hope that I might win my husband's confidence and trust again. But though he was calmer when I got home, I could see he was still angry. Nothing I said could make him see anything from my perspective. For several weeks after that, I carried the burden of guilt as I tortured myself with what I had considered doing and the price that might have paid on my already flagging marriage. I could not fathom how on earth Anthony could ever have found out, since I had only shared my plans with his sister. She was my best friend and had empathised with me so much, I did not believe it could have been her. Clutching at straws, I considered that one of my new Internet friends might have called Anthony, but of course none of them had our number, so I had to dismiss that. It was possible that Anthony had gained access to my Internet account and found out that way. Finally, he told me that his sister had called him that morning when I was heading into town because she thought he should know of my planned liaison. She had thought that it might help to repair our broken marriage if Anthony were aware of my plans. Her actions though, had broken my confidence and our friendship was sent into as much turmoil as my marriage, as she allowed her brother to know all of the secret fantasies I had shared only with her. It was heartbreaking as I discovered the beautiful rose that I had adored for years had a stem of invisible thorns.

⋆ ⋆ ⋆

Jesus was let down by many. He spent His life loving everyone faithfully, but even His own disciples were unable to stand by Him always. Peter denied even knowing Him because he was afraid of the consequences, but the ultimate betrayal was unquestionably that of Judas Iscariot who turned his Lord over to the chief priests. He may have done this through greed, or it may have been fear as he cracked under the pressure, but it is significant perhaps that in Matthew's

Gospel he does not convey Judas's motives. Instead, he allows us to consider the many reasons why anyone would betray in such a way. In general we tend to hold harsh judgment against those who betray us. Trust is a critical element in any relationship and betrayal will quickly shatter the bonds that hold it together. Once Judas realised the gravity of what he had done, he was filled with remorse, but this was too late. The consequences of his actions could not be turned around. Jesus would die, and unable to live with his guilt, so too would Judas. Did Jesus forgive him? I believe he did. In moments of weakness or before allowing enough time to think things through we can all be overwhelmed by fear or greed and inevitably create situations that we might well be remorseful for later. As Christians we are taught to follow Jesus' willingness to forgive, though it may not always be possible for us to forget. I doubt even Jesus did that. Once we have been sharply blistered by the prickly thorn on our roses, we continue to enjoy their blooms but learn to approach them with greater caution.

The friendships I made on the Internet served their purpose at a time when I most needed them, though they were never real. How could they be? The man who had shown me so much attention was never really interested in me. As soon as he learned that Anthony had discovered what I was planning he disappeared. He had suggested that he was in love with me, but love would have proved stronger than that. Though I did not need the complication of him continuing to pursue me once Anthony was aware of him, the realisation that his motives had only been sexual and that he had no genuine interest in me was almost as hurtful as when my sister-in-law broke my confidence. As soon as my life took a positive upturn, I recognised that most of the people I had befriended online had no more interest in me than I did in them. They were essential at a time when I was vulnerable and needy. I have no regrets about those shallow friendships, but I learned that the Internet is not a place to build true, constructive relationships, particularly when we are fragile. With almost everyone involved having their own individual issues as well as the dishonest character who preys on the vulnerable, all too often such chat rooms can complicate a situation further still.

In time I forgave my sister-in-law for betraying my trust. Although I will never be sure, I chose to believe that she did what she did for what she believed were the right reasons. It wasn't easy, but we pulled our friendship back together and for a while we remained close. Inevitably after Anthony and I divorced we also drifted, but I had loved her for many years so the fragrance of our friendship will always be with me.

Anthony caused me surmountable heartache both during our marriage and for some time after. For a long time after we separated I remained wounded with an inner anger. There then came a time when I realised that I was no longer hurting and as that pain subsided so did any hidden resentment towards him. I have some fond memories of the time we spent together. In a twenty year relationship of course there were happy times. Ultimately, my children, and now my beautiful grandchildren, are a wonderful consequence of our marriage and I am thankful for the love that I have through them. However, to spare being pricked by any remaining sharp thorns that Anthony might still have, I choose not to see him at all these days. Instead I only need to think of the things that caused me to love him, and I now actually enjoy the faded fragrance of the time we spent together.

STAY OUT OF THE SHADOWS

Forget the former things; do not dwell on the past.
See, I am doing a new thing!
Isaiah 43v18-19 NIV

One of our greatest hurdles as we attempt to move forward from our past wounds is not fully letting go of them. When a long term pattern is broken, it can be hugely daunting to consider coping with day-to-day life in a different way. That familiar way of going about things may have become a great security to us over time. Considering a future without it and having to accept that the experiences of our past are gone (however difficult they may have been) can for a while be overwhelming.

Sometimes it is the devastating pain of learning to live without a loved one who has died that can leave us feeling so lost and alone. At such a time, it is a normal human emotion to feel consumed with all sorts of negative feelings, including regret and guilt as well as those of sadness and emptiness from the loss. Having to face up to the reality that life will be a different journey without them can be very frightening and one that we are often reluctant to face.

The thin line between wonderful memories and accepting reality can be difficult to balance, though essential to work out in order to regain a healthy equilibrium for the future. Guilt can switch itself on quickly as we reminisce, and there is a temptation to dwell on the past and that which cannot be changed instead of preparing ourselves for the future and accepting that it will be different. Guilt feelings, particularly about the idea of a life without the one who has passed on, are often unjustified and have no relevance in helping to make way for the new future. By learning to move forward we do not lose any of the love we have felt before. In time, it is possible to rebuild from such a shattering experience without torturing ourselves that we may be letting the loved one down. A time must come when we have to accept their passing and look at all that life still has to offer us, even without them.

After a two year struggle with cancer Malc's first wife, Julie, lost her fight before she had reached the age of forty. The pain from his loss was obvious and understandable, but gradually he learned to accept her passing and realised he needed to love and share again. Though he had loved her wholly, he was also extremely lonely after her death and unable to contemplate spending the rest of his life without feeling such love again. When we first met, we discussed their relationship openly from the beginning, with great fondness and all the respect she deserved. We placed her photographs in our home as a fond memento, and we both believe that we have been able to reach a healthy balance of letting her go and keeping her memory alive. Malc has managed to move out of the cold shadows and draw warmth from the sun again.

My birth mother lost her second husband when she was still a young woman having just turned 50. As with Malc, the circumstances were extremely tragic and understandably difficult for her to come to terms with. For many years after he died, each New Years Eve, which was the anniversary of his passing, we would gather as a family and reminisce fondly over the person we had known as well as listen to my mother relive every detail of the awful day when we had lost him. For many, many years, the New Year celebrations were marred with tears instead of laughter, and it became difficult to find a reason to celebrate.

More than twenty years on, though the tears have faded, my mother still finds life incredibly difficult without him. Her life is often lonely, though she vows she will never re-marry if for no other reason than to take his name to her own grave. Such a sad admission only emphasises that she continues to live in the shadows without the courage to emerge fully from them.

We often hear or use the words, "They would want you to move on and be happy", when we attempt to comfort someone who has suffered such a loss. The reality is true. Those who had truly loved us would not want or expect us to spend our lives being miserable after their passing. There is no benefit to putting our life on hold. Instead we would do better to reach a healthy balance of grieving and sadness and then accepting that although our loved ones are gone from us, we are still very much alive! It is imperative for our own healthy living that we find the right level of mourning as well as understanding how to continue.

The same principles will apply if our loss is due to the breakdown of a relationship, whether it be a marriage, a friend or another family member. Such a crumbling of something that had felt secure for a long time can fill us with a sense of mourning. The consequences are often similar to that of a death. A long term relationship naturally draws us towards a certain amount of dependency on each other. When that bond is severed it can leave a void which is filled by fear as we contemplate the adjustments we will need to make through our separation. The history we have built with each other will bring many memories to the surface. Some will be good and some not so good, and the prospect of no longer having that love in our life can be worrying and frightening. Often, this daunting idea can interfere with us reaching a realistic or inevitable conclusion.

★ ★ ★

In a similar way to 'pruning off the dead wood', it is important not to look back from a decision once we have made it. That can be a tough call when we are torn and confused. However difficult life became for me at the end of my first marriage, I still loved Anthony. Even once I knew in my heart that the marriage was over, the idea of voluntarily taking myself away from everything I had known for the past twenty years seemed unthinkable and incredibly frightening. I had become so familiar with my surroundings and circumstances that I could not visualise a life outside of that institution. I felt more comfortable sitting in the shade than the idea of basking in the sun!

Despite everything, there was still a bond between us, but the way we demonstrated our love was very different. I am a natural giver, and in addition to that I also have an 'all or nothing' approach to much of what I come across in life. My critics would suggest that I am greatly 'black and white' about matters. Often situations are either one thing or another with me, and I tend to be blind to anything in between, with no room for grey areas. Sometimes that can be seen as a failing, but I am more inclined to consider it a strength. In relationships and my workplace, I either give all or I give nothing and so you will always know where you are with me. Anthony on the other hand is greatly consumed by his own needs and the things that he likes to do. For much of the time I had not fully recognised the extent of that. But even from the beginning, he made it clear that being married and having a family would not restrict him from doing the same things he had enjoyed as a single man. I quickly learned to accept that, but in doing so I left myself open for a great deal of hurt and loneliness over the years. Finally though, I accepted that the blemishes within our relationship had become far too deep to restore and I knew the only way forward for me was to leave.

Even after I had recognised that need, and having taken the necessary action, what proved to be almost impossible in the beginning was actually teaching myself to let go of my past and reach out to all that lay ahead. For the first two years after leaving Anthony, I clearly did not manage to do that. Despite finding myself in a new and far more fulfilling relationship within a few months, I continued to carry the heavy 'guilt burden' in my rucksack. In those early days, when I was still weak and vulnerable, Anthony was able to play endless mind games with me in the same way that I had allowed him to throughout our marriage. My reaction to these emotional games only aided in allowing him to load up the rucksack further still, sapping even more of my mental strength.

These endless guilt trips caused me such mental confusion that often I found it difficult to believe or accept that my life would ever be better, even with Malc. For a long time, I hindered any opportunity for this new relationship to develop because I wouldn't or couldn't completely let go of the past. I sat back in the shade and allowed the shadows to dampen my spirits again.

Making decisions as poignant as those I made take immense strength. Many times people told me how brave I was to have walked away. In the early days when my self-esteem was low, their words, which were meant as compliments to my character or moral support, actually had the reverse effect. In my low ebb I would question what exactly had been so brave about splitting up my family. I felt incredibly selfish when I considered how positive my new life had become, while my husband's life had fallen apart and my children were suffering intense confusion. Then I would beat myself up, believing I should have stayed and tried harder to make it work. Leaving the children was 'brave' my friends would tell me, but that was what I questioned most of all. I would spend endless hours wondering if those same people actually despised me for what I had done. In those days, I still placed far too much emphasis on what other people thought of me instead of considering my own feelings and the decisions I had made.

For a long time I was unable to fathom out a healthy balance over my actions. Once I moved in with Malc I found myself in a situation that gave me everything I had ever yearned for, but living without the children was unbearable and remains today the most painful decision I have ever made. I don't regret that I have pulled my life around and discovered who I really am, but I will always regret the impact it caused my children and the amount of time that was needed to restore our relationship. Even though by the time I moved away from them they were stretching into young independent people, and it would have been unfair to uproot them or separate them from the life they knew, in those early days I was consumed with guilt that I had left them behind and was beginning to enjoy an otherwise stress free life. I became very conscious of the choice my birth mother had made when I was such a small child, and those thoughts filled me with remorse as I considered that my decision might have caused similar turmoil for my own children. Unlike my mother, my maternal bond was, and remains unbreakable. My love for those two beautiful people is such that only I can fully understand. To this day, raising those two precious gifts has given me my greatest sense of pride. Nothing can ever surpass it.

Finally, as my strength began to recover, I accepted my decision and the reasons that I had needed to make it. It had been made only to preserve my sanity, nothing else. And I understood that for that reason, it had been a wise choice, not just for myself, but also for my children, and even my first husband. The plans that my children were beginning to make, would have come together whether I had stayed with Anthony or not. Then, as they reached full maturity and flew the nest completely, I would have become even more isolated in a loveless marriage, and the consequences would have drained my confidence even further. Continually questioning a decision that I had concluded was right at the time would not change anything other than risk the peace of mind I was beginning to discover.

Dale Carnegie is the author of *How To Stop Worrying And Start Living*. My dad had given me a copy of it as a birthday gift several years earlier. I admit that at the time I had paid little attention to it and had even thought it was a little strange to present me with such a book at all. In hindsight, he was probably aware even then that my character had changed considerably over the years and had an idea that there was tension in my life. As parents, we have earned that great gift of hindsight which we can use fruitfully for the benefit of our children. Having already made the mistakes we see them capable of making, we can offer our own experiences in the hope that they might choose not to repeat our earlier errors. I know now that my dad was more aware of my circumstances than I realised, though he chose not to interfere openly. The book was surely a gentle nudge!

I finally took to reading my book just a few months into my new life. Once I got started I found it difficult to put it down. It was a great source of encouragement, which provided me with some great counselling. Malc and I began reading it together, and with his wonderful understanding of my complex character at that time, he was able to recognise all sorts of patterns in my behaviour and what was causing them. The book became a major turning point in helping me take small steps away from the shadows of my past.

I learned that the only way I could successfully deal with my issues, while I was still riding the emotional roller coaster, was to take one or two problems at any time and concentrate only on them. It was a great discipline because I naturally wanted everything to fix itself at once. However, with so much to overcome, it would have been impossible to take everything on at the same time.

I learned to create imaginary boxes in my head. Then I put each problem into an individual box and closed the lid. By mentally imagining that scenario, I was able to switch off from anything I had tucked away, only having to concentrate on what remained. This exercise was amazingly easy to carry out once I had mastered it, and it allowed me to work through each problem thoroughly. The situation I remember most clearly was with one of the many heated arguments between my daughter and I. Weary and mentally unable to deal with my thoughts in the aftermath, I closed my eyes and watched myself lift her up and gently tuck her into a box. I then sat on it and sealed down the lid with tape, all in my head. By carrying out this mental exercise I was actually able to clear the argument completely from my mind and I left her in the box for several weeks while I dealt with something else. Today, my problems are usually less serious, but I still use that same technique in order to work things out in a structured manner. By entering anything in a muddled, unplanned way we will not have the clarity needed in order to deal with it appropriately and move forward from it.

★ ★ ★

During the time I have been writing this book, the Lord has led me to many people who I have later discovered could benefit greatly from reading even a few chapters from it. So many of the people I have met (some of them have become close friends), have experienced situations not so different from those I have known. Too often, instead of acknowledging their circumstances, they sadly consider their cup as half empty and fall into the unhealthy trap of self-pity or resolution only because they don't understand how to make healthy, positive changes. In order to make such decisions the cup needs to be seen as half full. Positives need to be recognised. I have no shame in sharing my intimate experiences with any of my friends or those who I believe would benefit from hearing them, and I hope that this book will stretch into the wider world and give inspiration to those that I or God would otherwise have never reached. I pray that I have used the words God has given me clearly to demonstrate the importance of tending each area of the life garden tentatively but thoroughly. From establishing the root causes right through to loving your beautiful lawn, each and every chapter is significant in creating a delightful and fruitful garden.

I could not have imagined the amount of time and tears it would take in order to make the weeds and worms manageable once I had disturbed my deep and forgotten roots. Today they are still with me, but with much thanks to my loved ones and my own courage, they only appear in my life long enough to remind me not only of where I have been but also where I have come to. I am thankful that they haven't disappeared completely because they help to keep me grounded and appreciate the wonderful way my life has changed.

In sifting through the debris of my broken emotional wall I discovered strengths that I might not otherwise have acknowledged. Within that clean-up operation, I was able to let go of anything that was no longer functioning by pruning the dead wood on my branches and allowing new growth for my future. Thus discarding what was no longer useable by tying it into bin bags, or recycling on the compost heap anything which would provide me with strength in the future.

God made us man and woman in order that we should demonstrate our love both mentally and physically. Because of the way he made us, it is natural and right for us to desire one another physically within a loving relationship. The shame I had felt when Anthony refused to love me in this way was unfounded, and by discovering the birds and the bees in my garden, I overcame the humiliation and embarrassment of my desires to be loved.

Creating a resourceful water butt and living within my means has given me peace of mind knowing that I have something aside for a dry spell (no matter how small). Where finances are really stretched, professional advice would be far more useful than to continue spending freely money which is not affordable. I have established that whilst having an income and enough money is important, it should never be allowed to become the greatest force within our lives.

Collectively, as I have tended each area of my life I have recognised the importance of spending time considering my own personal needs, however hectic life is. Loving your lawn is essential in order to enjoy the garden fully. Spending just a small amount of time on yourself will raise your self-esteem and ensure that you feel more worthy. Though I might handle them with caution for fear of an unexpected thorn, I have learned how to sit back and smell the roses. Finally I am conscious that most flowers develop better in the warmth of the sun rather than the shade. In the same way we must not hide ourselves under the clouds of our past, but instead embrace the light of our positive changes joyfully. When all is done in that wonderful life garden, sit back, 'keep your eyes always towards the sunshine and let the shadows fall behind you'!

REECE

The Lord does not look at the things man looks at. Man looks at the outward appearance, but the Lord looks at the heart.

1 Samuel 16v7 NIV

I have seen many people walk with me through my life in one way or another, and have gained greatly from family and friends who have proved to be hardy perennials and have remained with me during all weathers. They have provided me with a continued splash of fragrance to lift my spirits throughout low times and have been a joyous blessing that I have been able to depend on as they greatly enrich my life.

Those of my long term friends and family who through circumstances and logistics are not always close at hand I have chosen to think of as the bi-annuals in my life garden. These relationships are equally precious as they provide a well rooted and established friendship with a reassurance that they are never completely out of reach, even though the seasons of life have taken them in other directions for a while. I have one particular set of friends, a husband and wife who I have known since school. Over many years, we have shared incredible joys and heartaches as our lives have both seen different but equally difficult turbulent storms. For several years now they have been living overseas, which has made it difficult to keep up a regular friendship. When they do come home nowadays, their main priority is to spend time with their growing family. Nevertheless, when we do get together, it as if we have never been apart. I can't call them my best friends; I have so many other friends who are incredibly special in my life. However, these two people are the friends that I have known the longest and I would never want to have to consider a time when they might leave my life for good. They are bi-annuals, springing into life every now and then and bringing with them an abundance of love and joy each time they appear. Though their flowers wither and fade for a while as they tend their own life garden, I am never without confidence that another bloom will emerge as the seasons turn again, and I wait with anticipation for that time.

Then there are those whom I consider as annuals. These are the people who touch my life only briefly. The bloom may be full and bright for a while through the season, but when the flowers fade they are not likely to return. This might be a person I have met through another friend, or perhaps sat next to on a bus and passed the time of day with. Even someone who has touched my heart through the media as I have listened to a touching testimony has provided me with a fragrance of learning and empathy for a while as I consider their circumstances. However, no one person has ever left me with the same delicate scent as a small boy I shared lunch with one day in Cardiff. He will have brushed passed me without ever knowing quite how he had affected me that day.

It was about eighteen months after my marriage breakdown, and during a time when the relationship between me and my daughter was particularly fragile. Both of us were hurting and as a consequence of our pain, we were also angry. My daughter and I have very different ways of venting our anger, and because of that we are often frustrated by each other. Whilst I am normally fairly restrained in what I say, even in anger, my daughter tends to verbally lash out in an attempt to 'hit the spot'. In those early days before I had gained the strength I am now blessed with, such disturbing and volatile confrontations would have pushed me into a depressive state, and I would have spent hours or even days alone on my bed in a pathetic heap hoping that a miracle would occur and change everything around again. In depressed isolation, I would hope and pray that she would come to recognise my pain and at least acknowledge her own part in our conflict instead of assuming all faults to be down to me. My daughter finds it difficult to apologise, and therefore the only way a situation was normally resolved is to let it pass as though it has never happened.

One day while Malc and I were in Cardiff on business, my daughter and I had another furious fight over the telephone. As usual, I ended up in a flood of inconsolable tears, and by the time Malc left for his business meeting I was greatly distressed, as was he. In recent months there had been many furious arguments between us, but that morning she became particularly spiteful and afterwards I found it difficult to switch off from her angry outburst.

The visit to Cardiff had been long planned, and I had been looking forward to spending the day in the city centre, shopping and treating myself to a nice lunch while Malc attended his meeting. The fight with my daughter left me feeling so miserable that instead of the enjoyable day I had planned, I drifted around aimlessly, reliving everything that we had said to each other over and over in my mind, beating myself up and with no interest in the shops at all.

After wandering for some time without purpose or the ability to switch off, I came across a church just off the main High Street. At that time, I was still re-acquainting with God and had only recently had the courage to go back to church. In my mind I was still building bridges with Him, since I believed that He would find it hard to forgive me for breaking up my marriage. Nonetheless, I was compelled to go in and sit quietly for a while. For several minutes I sat motionless and staring at the crucifix ahead of me. I felt fraudulent and lost, unable to fully understand my compulsion to be there.

The church was beautiful and peaceful. The architecture was several hundred years old, and its stillness and tranquillity offered warmth and homeliness. After a while I closed my eyes and opened myself up in prayer. I didn't understand how to talk to God at first, but gradually I asked Him to provide me with guidance and understanding towards my daughter as well as the strength I needed to pull myself through this traumatic time with her. The more I prayed, the more my emotions bubbled up inside of me until I became a pathetic state of uncontrollable tears.

With my head in my hands and sobbing relentlessly, I became aware that I was no longer alone, and as I looked up I discovered the church minister had sat beside me. He smiled gently and asked if I would like to share my troubles with him. I felt somewhat pathetic to unravel my complications to a person I had never met before, but slowly and candidly I began to explain why I was so miserable. Little by little, I explained my fear of losing my daughter and grandson forever because we were unable to discuss our issues without fighting. After a while it became easier to offload and having him there beside me to listen provided me with great comfort.

The minister was an American man who had taken up his post in Cardiff only the summer before. As he began to understand what I was telling him, he related my circumstances to those of the transition he had needed to make when he had taken up his new post. He told me how much he had enjoyed tending his garden in America and that he had even brought with him some trees to plant.

"I have been greatly impatient while I have waited for those trees to mature," he said, "but I have needed to learn to understand that they will not mature overnight. I have to sit back and wait patiently and try to enjoy each stage of their development until they reach maturity. In a similar way, your daughter is just like my trees. You want her to mature and blossom to your new situation right away, but she needs time to adjust and understand it. She isn't able to accept your new circumstances immediately because she needs time to work them out for herself." I soon began to understand what he was saying to me and realised I had never looked it from such an angle before. We continued to talk for several minutes and, as my tears began to dry up, I felt humbled that a man who didn't know me and who owed me nothing would take the trouble to offer such sensible advice in order that I could work things through. "Sometimes the answers we are given are not what we expect or even what we want to hear," he continued, "that's when we need to hold on to our faith and accept that God is working for us as we sift our way out of the wilderness of our confusion."

Surprisingly, the minister's words did manage to provide some comfort, though possibly, and, like he had said himself, not all of his words were ones I was hoping to hear. I am not sure I knew what I wanted to be told, I just wanted the pain to leave me, and for my daughter and I to be friends again. However, in my heart, and beneath my grieving, I knew that everything he said to me was logical and made sense. My daughter and I both needed time to adjust to our new circumstances, before we could expect to have the fruitful and functioning relationship that I yearned for.

My daughter had just become a young mother at the tender age of nineteen. The pressures of that, together with learning to accept that her parents had separated, must have been more than a little overwhelming to her. I had not fully considered the strain that she had been under during this time because I had been so focused on my new circumstances with Malc, and restoring my confidence. In addition I was also trying desperately to form a relationship with my new grandson. Considering her needs as well as my own, helped me to disperse some of my anger and frustrations towards her, and thus find a more sympathetic approach towards her. What it didn't do was take away the sickening dread in my stomach that, if in the end we were unable to work through our differences sensibly, I might lose her completely.

The minister and I held hands and prayed together. As I left the church I kissed him gently on the cheek and thanked him for his words of hope and encouragement. I knew I would never see him again, but he had been greatly supportive at a time when I was in desperate need of it. He would be an annual in my life garden. Though he was a bloom that was bright and fragrant for a short while, once gone he would not return. His job was done. He had brightened a dark and dreary place in perfect timing and would leave an impression for a long time going forward.

After leaving the church, and having wandered around the shops for a while mulling over the advice I had been given, I realised I was hungry. I had originally planned to find a nice bistro or wine bar to have lunch in so I could sit and read my book, but despite the encouraging time in the church I had not managed to fully snap out of my depression and so such a luxury lunch no longer appealed to me. Instead, I wandered aimlessly into a McDonalds. Having recently lost three stone, McDonalds was no longer a place I frequented, but I decided that for once it would not hurt and it was merely a means to an end.

Anyone who is a regular visitor to McDonalds in a hectic shopping centre will know how busy a place it can be. Cardiff was no exception. The place was heaving. People were queuing and pushing past to find a seat or just to reach the napkins and straws. Once I had paid for my meal, I had the same task as everybody else. There didn't seem to be a single spare seat available. Just as I was contemplating walking upstairs to see if it was less crowded there, I saw two people leave their table, and I quickly made my way towards the available seat.

As I sat down, I glanced at the little boy who was occupying the seat next to mine. Pulling off my jacket, I accidentally knocked him with my arm and immediately turned to apologise to him. It was then that I noticed he was quite small and about five or six years old. At the same time I also noticed that his arms and hands were quite severely twisted with big lumps appearing above his wrists. Quite politely he told me that he was okay and I smiled gently but quickly looked away from him, not wanting to appear as if I was shocked by his obvious disability. As I sat quietly eating my burger, it was impossible not to notice that this little boy was incredibly well behaved and polite. In fact, I found the conversations he was having with his mummy greatly intriguing. Once or twice I glanced up and smiled in a friendly way to them both, but I was very aware of his handicap, and didn't want either of them to think it bothered or shocked me.

After a while he needed to blow his nose and he asked his mummy if she had a tissue. When she shook her head, I offered him one from my bag. Once again, very politely he thanked me, then tidied his nose and put the tissue in his pocket. I soon realised that I had become far more interested in this little boy's good manners than

I was by his handicap. Because his hands were unable to grip the chips very well, it was a painstaking operation for him to actually feed himself. I greatly admired his mummy's patience as well as her understanding of his need for independence as she allowed him to feed himself without any help from her. The difficulties he had to actually get the chip to his mouth might have tempted her to do it for him, but clearly he was used to this exercise and got on with it without complaint.

I noticed that the woman wasn't eating, and assumed at first that she had already finished her lunch. That would have made sense given that it was taking such a long time for the little lad to munch his way through his food, but then I heard the little boy speak to her and I realised that she hadn't yet eaten.

"I'm sorry I'm so slow, Mummy", he said to her in his broad welsh accent, "but when I've finished eating my chips, we can go wherever you like so you can have some lunch."

"It's okay", she replied with a gentle smile, "I'm in no hurry. You just enjoy what you're eating. We have plenty of time".

Something else that was prolonging his meal was that every chip he took from the packet, needed to be dipped into a carton of ketchup before he ate it. This process took great skill on his part with his little arms being so crooked. However, eventually the carton of ketchup was empty and his mummy got up to go and fetch him some more. While she was gone, he confidently turned to talk to me.

"I love chips," he began confidently, "but I like them best when I can dip them in some ketchup."

"I like ketchup too," I lied with a warm smile, "what's your name?"

"Reece," he answered proudly. Then as if to confirm any reason for his parent's choice of name for him he added, "I'm Welsh."

"Yes, I can tell," I grinned. "And how old are you then, Reece?"

"I'm nearly twelve," he replied. I was rather shocked by this answer, because he really didn't look any older than five or six. I smiled at him again, but as I did, I tried to look more closely at him to see if maybe I had missed something when I had first assumed his age. But, on looking at him again, he still seemed far younger and smaller than his twelve years.

Then, as if reading my mind, he went on: "I know I look small and all that, and I've got these horrid lumps on my arms, but I really am nearly twelve."

Trying then to make sure I didn't make a remark that would sound patronising or inappropriate, I turned to him and very gently said: "You know what Reece, you're right, you are a bit small, but you are the most polite little boy I have seen in a long time, and that makes you very big in my book." The grin on his face was something I will not forget. He positively beamed at my compliment. As he continued to grin at me, his mother returned with the pot of ketchup. By now I had finished eating my lunch, so I sat there for a while chatting to him and his mother as he dipped his chips.

"I spell my name R E E C E," he informed me. "It's a Welsh name." He was an absolute delight to be with and it occurred to me that while we had been chatting, I had forgotten about the problems that had been lying so heavily on me all morning.

"I guessed you were probably Welsh, since we are in the centre of Cardiff!" I laughed. His proud remarks had really made me smile. We chatted for a few more minutes, but I had long finished eating my lunch and I didn't want to intrude on the intimate time he was sharing with his mother, and so as not to outstay my welcome, I got up to put on my jacket and say my goodbyes. I couldn't help thinking how this little boy had every reason to be fed up and hold a grudge against life. Yet he was as happy as anyone I had ever known. I had spent the morning consumed in my problems as if there seemed no clear light ahead for me, and yet mine were only within my family. Mine were problems of conflict and ones that could be resolved. Reece might spend his whole life needing to be acknowledged by society, but he gracefully took on that challenge. My own troubles suddenly appeared trivial by comparison.

"You know what Reece?" I said as I finished buttoning my jacket,

"I had a really bad morning, and when I came in here just now I was feeling rather fed up. But sitting and talking to you has been a privilege and has truly made my day. I feel so much brighter now. You are a remarkable little boy, have a great time this afternoon with your mummy, it has been so nice to meet you."

"It was nice meeting with you too." He smiled, "I'm glad I made your day." And I think he really was.

The brief time that I spent with Reece that day has played a significant part in my life since then. It demonstrated to me that though each of us have our own difficult situations to deal with, there is always someone else with a greater burden to come to terms with. Though he passed through my garden only once, the fragrance that he left behind remains with me today. Most of us are well aware that we are blessed in abundance, though sadly our complacency often leads us into taking such blessings for granted. Reece has been an obvious reminder to me that I am greatly gifted. During times when my spirits are low and I have a tendency to feel sorry for myself I think of him in order to gain perspective and rid myself of self pity. Reece doesn't feel sorry for himself because he can't have what he wants. I am sure that he would have preferred to be more like his friends, but instead he is different and accepts who he is gracefully. He gets on with his life and embraces what God has given him: a wonderful heart with tremendous inner confidence. He doesn't allow his disability and circumstances to dictate who he is, rather, he accepts them as part of who he will become.

Each of us can benefit from his wisdom.

RANDOM ACTS OF KINDNESS (UK)

Remember this; whoever sows sparingly, will also reap sparingly. And whoever sows generously will reap generously.

2 Corinthians 9v6 NIV

At the end of 2011, while hosting a small dinner party for the family of my great friend Carole Jenet, I learned about The Random Acts Of Kindness Foundation based in Denver Colorado. The idea of promoting kindness within the communities that we live in, deeply stirred me, and I set out to launch a similar ministry here in the UK.

On the 25th March 2012, with the support of our local church and full backing from our friends in Colorado, Random Acts Of Kindness (UK) was launched. Initially we expected to create subtle changes within our own community and encourage people to be more thoughtful and aware of each other's needs. However, in just a few weeks we had already mustered interest from around the UK and the wider world.

Very quickly we linked up with other similar organisations, and learned how collectively there is an opportunity to really make a difference within the communities that we live. By encouraging each other to demonstrate even the smallest gestures to one another, there is a real potential to create a gentler world. Our research has identified that most people enjoy being kind, but sadly we live in a world which is hungry for materialism and often living for the moment, that kindness often loses its way. Kindness can be spread in all number of ways and becomes infectious both for the giver and the recipient. An unexpected kind gesture melts away anger and hostility, being replaced by a warm, inner glow.

Many people have shown a lot of unkindness towards me through the years, usually to fulfil their own needs of control and often without me even knowing. Having lived through such times, I believe that many situations such as those I have known could be avoided if people were more willing to consider others as well as themselves. It might sound like an idyllic, tall order, and we are aware that change takes time and effort. However, we are currently working on programmes for young people in schools and youth groups, and are linked with many other charities and similar groups who share our ethos, and believe that collectively it is not just possible, but inevitable that change will happen.

For further information on the work of Random Acts Of Kindness (UK), you will find us at:

www.randomactsofkindnessuk.co.uk

or email us at

info@randomactsofkindnessuk.co.uk